Emily,
Praying for you
and am so happy
to have seen you
your family home in
Bengkulu!
Love Jana

Villa in the Hilla

Devotions from the Desert

By Jana Kelley

Dedication

This book is dedicated to the ladies who have adopted North Africa as their second home and have accepted the God-given tasks of raising their families, loving their neighbors and serving their Lord, even with dust in their hairlines and sweat on their brows. You are my sisters and my friends.

I love you!

CONTENTS

Preface

North Africa is a wonderful place to gather material for writing. During our time in that part of the world (which I shall, from here-on refer to as The Land of Sand) I enjoyed writing about what I saw and felt. I began writing about The Land of Sand through emails to family back home. Later, I contributed to a women's website and then to devotional books. The more I wrote, the more I found more to write about!

I always wanted to live outside the capital city, perhaps more for selfish reasons than anything. I thought it would be the greatest adventure of all and would provide me with more insights to write about. It was a big dream of mine. The Lord never gave me the opportunity to live far outside the city, but during our last year in The Land of Sand, we did rent a small house (villa!) in a small village ("hilla" in the language we learned) just outside the city. I began to joke that one day I would write my own book about The Land of Sand and call it "Villa in the Hilla."

For me, writing this little collection of "desert devotions" and naming it *Villa in the Hilla* is my "thank you" to the Lord for the wild ride of living in The Land of Sand for eight years and for His invitation to me (and all of us!) to continue to follow Him on the truly greatest adventure of all: His Will.

Villa in the Hilla

What's your "villa in the hilla"?
What's your greatest dream of all?
Can you hand it to your Savior?
Can you trust Him with your call?

Can you smile if it is different
Than what you had in mind?
Or harder than expected
With sorrows intertwined?

Do you dare think it could be better
Than what you thought to dream?
That in the end, the path He set
Is better than it seemed?

Give your "villa in the hilla"
To the Lord, and when you pray
Trust the twists and turns and all you learn
To the One Who knows the way.

Day 1: God's Precious Word

Your statutes are my heritage forever; they are the joy of my heart.

Psalm 119:111

Scripture has always been a large part of my life. I was raised on the nourishment of the Word daily. Before I even knew what it meant, I could quote the books of the Bible in order. My parents helped us children in memorizing verses. I wanted to read the Bible daily like my parents and older siblings did. I have been told that, in first grade, as soon as I learned to read my first word (which was the word "and") I would spend time each morning going through my Bible finding all the "and"s I could find. That was my daily time in the Word!

Scripture has always been important. I would say, though, that Scripture became "precious" to me in the Fall of 2001. My husband and I had just finished two years of intense language study and now we were headed to the country we felt God calling us to. We had shipped what little belongings we had ahead of us and had moved out of our house. Now we were staying just a few weeks in a guesthouse as we prepared to move to our new home. We were filled with excitement and anticipation. We were now face to face with what we had been working toward for years: making our home in North Africa. A week before our departure, we were invited to a colleague's house for a "going away" dinner. When we knocked on their door, we were met by the husband who quickly ushered us in and straight to the television where together we watched an airplane fly straight into one of the twin towers in New York. Was it true? I remember thinking the footage looked like a badly shot "B-rated" movie. It was unreal. Things happened fast and people all across the world panicked. Our move was put on hold.

For more weeks than we'd planned, we waited and watched to see what would happen. Would we get to go? Would our sending agency forbid us? For me it was an emotional time and a "step" of faith to not take any steps. I truly learned to wait on the Lord. I remember sitting out on the balcony of the guesthouse and reading Psalms. I just

1

devoured the words of David and his cries to the Lord sang the very words I couldn't express. That was when God's Word became precious to me.

As it turned out, we were delayed only about six weeks. I don't think it was a mistake that I began to hunger for His Word just weeks before we were able to move. I think it was a lesson the Lord wanted me to learn. Over the next eight years, His Word would become my life-line.

During dark seasons I would write out verses and post them all over the kitchen walls, the bathroom walls, the bedroom walls. Sometimes I had verses posted at our front gate or by the phone. Each verse posted meant something special to me for a particular time in my life that the Lord and I were working through. They became a reminder to me and a testimony to others of God's faithfulness.

Verses Posted in My Home

By my spice cabinet:

"Taste and see that the Lord is good; blessed is the man who takes refuge in Him." Psalm 34:8

On my children's bedroom door:

"I will lie down and sleep in peace, for you alone, O Lord, make me dwell in safety." Psalm 4:8

By my house phone:

"When words are many, sin is not absent, but he who holds his tongue is wise." Proverbs 10:19

By our front gate:

"The Lord will watch over your coming and going both now and forevermore" Psalm 121:8

In our bathroom (where I get ready in the mornings):

"Be our strength every morning, our salvation in time of distress." Isaiah 33:2

On my mirror:

"Your beauty should not come from outward adornment like braided hair and the wearing of gold jewelry and fine clothes. Instead it should be that of your inner self, the unfading beauty of a gentle and quiet spirit which is of great worth in God's sight." 1 Peter 3:3-4

Day 2: Refining Fire

These have come so that your faith-of greater worth than gold, which perishes even though refined by fire-may be proved genuine and may result in praise, glory and honor when Jesus Christ is revealed. 1 Peter 1:7

I keep a journal. I have since I was 8 years old. In my parent's attic back in Texas, I have a trunk full of journals that chronicle my life from a little town on the island of Java in Southeast Asia, to the Philippines, United States, through the Arab World, well, you get the idea. I like journaling because I can learn so much just by looking back at things that have happened. I have a journal entry from December 8, 2005 that reads,

"I've been able to look back at a couple of really hard months and see how much the Lord has taught me. I can feel how much He must love me to teach me so much. I really didn't like the difficulties, but I do like the results. If I can face the hard times with the knowledge and faith that nothing can permanently harm me, only burn off the dross, then I do not have to fear the fire. Thank you, Lord, for taking away not only the sting of death, but also the sting of Satan's arrows in life."

Some places and some situations in life are "refining fires." Do we let them burn off the dross, or do we let them harden our hearts? I can look back to times in my life and testify to what is said in Isaiah 48:10,

"See, I have refined you, though not as silver; I have tested you in the furnace of affliction."

I have certainly felt the flames of affliction, but, because I am God's child, I know they can never bring me harm. James 1:2-4 reads,

"Consider it pure joy, my brothers, whenever you face trials of many kinds, because you know that the testing of your faith develops perseverance. Perseverance must finish its work so that you may be mature and complete, not lacking anything."

What is your current refining fire, your current trial? Is it physical illness? Difficult living situation? Relationship problems? Ministry problems? Family problems? When you face trials in any form, you can know, even if you don't feel it emotionally, that this is a test of your faith in God's _____. You fill in the blank: His goodness, His plan, His control, etc. This pressure on your faith develops endurance in your spiritual muscles. If you let God use this period of time to complete your spiritual workout, the end result will be maturity in Him. And that truly is something to be joyful about!

It's not about us or our talents or limitations...

But the Lord said to me, "Do not say, 'I am only a child.' You must go to everyone I send you to and say whatever I command you. Do not be afraid of them, for I am with you," Jeremiah 1:7-8

What is your "I am only"?

"Do not say, 'I am only _____.' You must go to everyone I send you to and say whatever I command you. Do not be afraid of them, for I am with you."

What is the Lord saying to you about your

"I am only"s?

Day 3: The Criminal

For God so loved the world that he gave his one and only Son, that whoever believes in him shall not perish but have eternal life. For God did not send his Son into the world to condemn the world, but to save the world through him. John 3:16-17

"I'm not a goat! I'm a person! I'm not a goat! I'm a person!" I yell until my voice is hoarse, but no one pays any attention. But I AM a goat! I have speckled hair and horns on my head. I am surrounded by other goats who are scavenging around for bits of trash and old food. We are surrounded by a wire fence next to a brick building. I don't know where we are exactly, but I know the brick building is a slaughtering house. I grow short of breath. The goats around me become a blur. I think I might pass out from fear. How did I get here?

Then I remember. I killed a man. Before I was a goat, that is. Somehow, I was a man. But I was not a good man. I stole things, I was a liar and dishonest at work. I lost my temper many times. One day I got mad at a man in the market. I didn't stop myself from getting angry. I became more and more enraged. That night I went to the man's house. We got into a fight again and I hit him. I killed him. That's all I know. Then I became a goat. Now I am in this pen and they are going to slaughter me like the other goats!

"I'M NOT A GOAT!" I scream again. This time someone hears me. A man…no, two; they walk slowly over to where I am, which is as far away from the slaughter house as possible.

"We know you are not a goat," says one of the men. "But you are a very bad person. So we are going to kill you along with all of these goats. You are like a goat and you will be slaughtered like one!" He grabs my horns and begins to drag me alongside the fence toward the brick building.

I begin screaming again, but this time my words morph into the bleating of a goat. No one speaks to me again. I begin to cry.

7

Then I see a man appear and he is carrying a beautiful white lamb. The snowy coat of the lamb seems so out of place in this dirty, muddy pen of speckled goats. The man is talking to my executioner.

"I brought this lamb to be sacrificed on behalf of all these goats," says the man with the lamb.

The man holding my horns lets me go. I back away quickly, but I stay close by. I want to see what is going to happen. The two men who had spoken to me now spoke to the man holding the lamb. Then they take the lamb.

They don't take it to the brick building. They just begin to slaughter the lamb right there in front of the other goats and me. The lamb doesn't bleat or fight. The blood spills from the lamb, and when it hits the ground it pools into the shape of a cross.

Blood, blood, red blood. Suddenly, I opened my eyes. I am not a goat! I am not in a pen with other goats. I am in my bed. I have been dreaming! I catch my breath quickly. It has all been a dream. None of it is real. Except the part about me being a bad person. I am a bad person and I have done things that deserve jail. But I have not been caught.

I am not a goat. For that, I should be very grateful. But I cannot forget my dream. I need someone to tell me what it means. I need to find a Christian. I have seen crosses on Christian churches before. Surely a Christian could tell me the message of my dream.

****

That day at the market, I saw two men walking by. I did not recognize them but someone told me they were from out of town and that they preached about Jesus. I ran after them.

"If you are Christians," I said, as I ran up to them from behind, "then God has sent you here! Please help me understand my dream!"

And that is what they did. Beginning with John 3:16, they explained to me my need for a blood sacrifice and how Jesus was the perfect sacrifice for all time. I am no longer that goat, physically or spiritually. I have been redeemed! (*Based on a true story*)

A Tribute to Dust

And now: a tribute to the dust.
A poem, I feel here, is a must.
Now, do not feel so tearful just
Because we are covered up in dust.
There are some benefits, I trust,
That may just make you feel robust.
So do not let your mind combust
When looking 'round your house in disgust,
And crying at what seems so unjust,
(As if it were a breach of trust)
That in your house, you cleaned and fussed
But now I write your name in dust.
I feel you'll see, above discussed
You will not win; this fight's a bust.
So you will have to readjust
And change perspective, that's the thrust.
Just embrace the summer dust!

Day 4: What's My Role?

His divine power has given us everything we need for life and godliness through our knowledge of him who called us by his own glory and goodness.

2 Peter 1:3

Are you a nurse who longs to practice her skills? Are you a new mom who mostly just longs for a good night's rest? Do you love to make your house "homey" or are you itching to get out of your house and spend time with nationals? The Lord has created in each of us women unique talents and desires. All of us have a vision or goal of some sort. We are as varied as the colored scarves that cover the women around us. We can celebrate our differences by encouraging others and by taking joy in what the Lord has called us to do. To judge others or to compare ourselves, however, is to throw a wet blanket on our celebration. Each of us is different and each one of us can honor God in our own way.

I mentored one young single lady who was very gifted in evangelism. She loved the ladies around her and they loved her. She often double booked herself because of the many visiting appointments she would make. I had to remind her to take a day off each week. This young lady had a roommate. Her roommate was very quiet; perhaps what some would call a "loner." She had few national friends and did not speak the language well. She was a prayer warrior, however. She spent large portions of time in prayer for the people of the land and the believers who worked there. The lady I mentored once went on an extended trip to the village. Her roommate set her alarm clock to ring every couple of hours. Upon hearing the alarm, she would drop everything and pray. I was struck by the partnership these two ladies had. Neither one judged the other for being different than herself. They simply celebrated their differences by learning to work together for a greater good. Only in Heaven will we know the great results of this shy woman's prayers and this friendly woman's boldness in sharing.

I am the sort who likes to get out and visit. One evening, while visiting in the home of a fellow worker, I asked her, "How often do you get to visit with national ladies?" She paused from chopping vegetables at her kitchen table where we sat.

"I don't do any visiting," she replied. "I know many ladies want to learn the language and visit the people. I just want to make a happy home for my husband and children." I realized then that, though I had certain goals for my time, it might not be the same as someone else's. I was encouraged by the way this friend of mine was confident and secure in her role.

Do you ever wonder, "What in the world is my role here?" I did, and still do sometimes. As a lady living in a "man's world", I often felt pushed aside. Married ladies with children are often so busy with taking care of the home that there is not time for outside "ministry." Single ladies are often so busy with their jobs that they feel this same strain. I was encouraged by someone who has more experience than me. She said that during the times that are so busy it is helpful to choose one thing that is your main ministry. Like, for example, for a couple of years I taught a conversational English class one night a week. It didn't take much to prepare and it gave me one night a week to spend with national women, which is what I wanted to do. Another year I worked at our children's school. That gave me the chance to meet a lot of kids and a lot of parents. Finding my "one thing" worked great for me.

In the end, however we spend our time, whatever we find our role to be, the Bible gives us encouragement on how to be successful. "For this very reason, make every effort to add to your faith goodness; and to goodness, knowledge; and to knowledge, self-control; and to self-control, perseverance; and to perseverance, godliness; and to godliness, brotherly kindness; and to brotherly kindness, love. For if you possess these qualities in increasing measure, they will keep you from being ineffective and unproductive in your knowledge of our Lord Jesus Christ" (2 Peter 1:5-8).

Does God Really Hear?

Does God really hear my prayer?
What difference does it really make
If I, just one, should bow my head
And ask for lost souls to be saved?

What if I cry for Africa?
Or Asia is my tearful plea?
What if my heart breaks for a thousand orphans
I know I'll never even see?

Do those prayers count
On Heaven's part?
Or am I left with my tears, my words
And my broken heart?

I flip through pages of
The Ancient Book and there I read
Story after story
Of God's answers in time of need.

"God's Word affirms that He will hear,"
Says Hannah with her son.
"Do not believe your prayers are mute."
Says Hezekiah, the battle won.

Cornelius says "God heard my plea,"
Lydia and her prayer group too.
And Zechariah, while holding John
Says, "You better believe it's true!"

God's Word, sisters, shows it's true!
He saves His own from every land.
And prayer is God's way of loving YOU.
By letting you join in His plan.

Oh, pray by faith! Give a sacrifice
for fruit you may not ever see.
And claim His Word for the world
God is working in mightily!

An eternal investment is made through prayer
For countless lives are touched.
You won't look back on life and say,
"I wish I hadn't prayed so much"!

So, does God really hear your prayer?
Does it make a difference, friend?
Oh yes, He hears! Oh yes, prayer works!
Can I get an "Amen"?

Day 5: Thriving

The children of your people will live in security. Their children's children will thrive in your presence. Psalm 102:28 (NLT)

Don't you want to THRIVE and not just SURVIVE? There were many days sprinkled through my years in The Land of Sand that I was just struggling to keep myself from coming un-frayed in front of everyone! I was doing good to survive, but I really wanted to thrive. Here is what I wrote one day:

I am in my eighth year in The Land of Sand. I cannot muster up "love" for The Land of Sand. Some people say they love it here but I just can't agree. I don't. But I am happy here. I have been wondering how that can be. I am not always happy here, but for the most part I am. I still can't say that I love it here. Is that OK? I have been asking the Lord lately.

Often I have prayed, "Lord, release us from The Land of Sand! Let us go!" But I always tell Him that I want His will over mine. And He still hasn't let us go. Why would He want me in a place that I don't love? I suppose it is not so much that I don't like it here, as much as the absence of loving it here. Is there a difference? I think so. The other day I read Psalm 102:28, "The children of your people will live in security. Their children's children will thrive in your presence." It occurred to me that many of us are grasping for handles on how to "not just survive but thrive" in The Land of Sand. Yes, I am physically in The Land of Sand, but I should spend my efforts learning to "thrive in (His) presence". I began to think of what I would miss if I left The Land of Sand. To be honest, I would not miss the food, I would not miss the heat, the dirt, the desert (even though it is beautiful), and I am not sure I would miss the people all that much, because everywhere there are people to be loved and who need to hear the Gospel. There is nothing I adore about the culture here. What would I miss? I would miss the unity of believers in Christ. I would miss the way this place requires me to be spiritually disciplined on a daily (no, on an hourly) basis. I would miss the deep friendships of fellow workers struggling in a difficult place. I

14

would miss hearing first-hand stories of national believers who are suffering for the sake of Christ. I would miss the deep spiritual lessons and growth that the Lord has brought me through during some really dark days in The Land of Sand. If I had not come to The Land of Sand, I would not be the person I am today. I am better, I am stronger and I am deeper in Christ. I rely more fully on Him for the very next breath that I take, and I learned that through a particularly difficult time in The Land of Sand. I crave His Word more deeply and I learned that through my time in The Land of Sand. I am more disciplined and more obedient to Christ. I relish His gifts more and I take His instruction more seriously. All of these are things I learned in The Land of Sand. I am learning to thrive in God's presence. If I can thrive in God's presence and, in His strength, live in The Land of Sand, then I can thrive in The Land of Sand. Not because I love The Land of Sand but because I love HIM. Recently, a friend of mine said, "If you are wondering if all your struggles in The Land of Sand are worth it, they aren't. The Land of Sand is not worth it. But Christ is worth everything, so Christ is worth it!" Amen sister! Christ is worth everything to me, so I will live in The Land of Sand and I will thrive in God's presence. There is nothing aesthetically pleasing about The Land of Sand that holds me here, but God has not released me from The Land of Sand and I will not let go of God, so I will trust Him and stay here as long as He wants me here. I will not just "grin and bear it" because that would not be thriving in Christ. I need to let go of my desire to love the physical side of The Land of Sand and I will just love Christ. I think that if people ask me, "Do you love it here?" I can honestly say, "I am happy here." And that comes from thriving in His presence.

Thriving...

"I love it there!" I hear them share
and then I wonder why
Can I not love it where I live, hard as I may try?
My mind goes back to former days
in lovelier places along the way.
Mountains high, trickling streams,
green is everywhere is seems.
Food is tasty, can't get enough.
Places like that are easy to love.
"Ah for a home... like that!" I groan.

The smell of trash, it brings me back
to where I've set up home.
Stray dogs have been in the garbage again
and now look what they have done!
The land is flat, the heat extreme,
there is no nice aesthetic theme.
Sometimes I want to scream, "Enough!"
This place is really hard to love!
"Is it ok?" I want to say,
when I'm alone and bow to pray.

It seems I work and pray and give
all toward the task for which I live.
If I pour myself into all I do,
surely love for this place will follow too?
But it never comes and I'm the one
left to wonder what's to be done.
Until I read His Word and see
a little treasure just for me!
"Thrive in His presence," that's the call,
nothing about the place at all!

"Thrive in His presence," I hear Him say.
It echoes all throughout the day.
So…I would say: I'm happy here;
but it's because the Lord is near.
And it's because of lessons learned
and tasty morsels from His Word.
And it's because life here is hard
so I rely just on the Lord.
And in the end, and it's a fact:
I'm glad I have a home like that!

Day 6: 2 Corinthians 4…The Way I See It

Dear friends, do not be surprised at the painful trail you are suffering, as though something strange were happening to you. But rejoice that you participate in the sufferings of Christ, so that you may be overjoyed when his glory is revealed.

1 Peter 4:12-13

There are times in my life when the Father repeatedly brings me to the same passage of Scripture. It may be a selection of verses that I have read over and over from the time I was a young child. Other times, it seems as if the verses are brand new, and I wonder how it is that I have read the Bible multiple times but still don't remember them. I dwell on a passage and I keep rereading it and when I hear it pop-up in conversations or sermons, I just smile. It is as if God is sending me little reminders that He still wants me to camp out in that chapter or verse of the Bible! 2 Corinthians 4 became that for me during a time when I was attempting to encourage a group of young people who were serving in The Land of Sand. I spent time reading and thinking about the chapter. Here is how I paraphrased it:

Since it is because of God's mercy that we are even here in The Land of Sand, we will not become discouraged when our circumstances become discouraging. Instead, we will focus on presenting the truth of Christ plainly to our friends. Then, if the truth is unclear, it is not because of us but because Satan has blinded them. For us, our conscience will be clear because we will be careful to always share Christ with everyone. We won't try to make others like us, but rather work to draw others to Christ through knowing us. God made light shine out of darkness and He made light shine in our hearts. We know He can also make His light shine in the hearts of the people.

God chose to put His wonderful treasure in fragile vessels. We are sick, we are tired, we are weak, we are homesick, and we are young. We are those fragile vessels carrying the amazing miracle of God in our very bodies! It is obvious to us that the

18

power is God's and not ours. We will not try to make it ours. We feel stress on every side (physical, emotional, relational and spiritual) but we will not let it crush us. We don't often understand why things happen the way they do, but we will choose not to be depressed or gloomy about it. We have been and will continue to be wronged by the enemy, but God will be with us through it all and we choose to keep our hand in His hand. Even if we fall, we will not lose because we are on God's side and His side wins!

We believe in Christ, His death and resurrection. We will let the Truth burn within us so that we cannot help but share it with everyone. The gospel is reaching more and more people and we choose to be a part of that and let the glory be God's alone.

Because of all this, we will not be afraid. Even if we are sick, tempted, fussy, tired, homesick, or wondering what will happen next, we choose to remember that it was God's mercy that called us here in the first place and it is His mercy that will see us through the weeks ahead. We choose to be renewed daily in His Word. The troubles we have now are short and easy, compared to the eternal difference that our time here will make for us (because we have grown so much in our faith) and for others (because of the eternal life they now have the chance to receive). So we choose to FIX our eyes on Jesus. We will not just glance at Him or occasionally remind ourselves of His presence, but truly be fixated on Jesus Christ. We will fix our eyes on the unseen; we will take our eyes OFF the seen. What is seen is temporary, just a shadow. What is unseen is eternal, it will be our reality.

Hard & Soft

Tough brown skin, wrinkled and scarred
From years of work and a life that was hard.
Oh the stories I might tell, if only I could.

My gnarled, arthritic and calloused hands
Brush back hair streaked with silvery strands.
Oh the stories I'd tell, and maybe I should.

My eyes are cloudy and vision is low
My voice is rough and words come slow.
I wonder if anyone would care to hear.

My body is bent and strength is gone.
But there is hope in this little one.
And that is why I hold him dear.

Healthy and new is his soft shiny skin.
His years are before him: a life to begin!
Just holding him seems to give life back to me.

Active and wiggly hands and feet
Clamber and grasp with energy sweet.
I wonder what he will grow up to be.

His eyes are black and bright as stones
As if ready to take on all the unknowns.
And, who knows? Maybe he really can.

Soft curls cover his little round head.
He is the hope after my life is led.
I felt free to go when his life began.

But holding him now, I have to resign
That his life will be just as hard as mine.
What will his choice be when life turns sour?

20

Right now he is soft but scars are in store
That may mar his skin and his heart even more.
Will he have the strength in his toughest hour?

Ah, to share my experience, that is my dream,
To help this boy build his strength and esteem.
To tell him who and what and where...

But that's not real life, not if I give it.
Life is experience, you have to live it.
So I hold him close and whisper a prayer.

Day 7: Little Disciples

For I am the Lord, your God, who takes hold of your right hand and says to you, "Do not fear; I will help you." Isaiah 41:13

So do not fear, for I am with you; do not be dismayed, for I am your God. I will strengthen you and help you; I will uphold you with my righteous right hand. Isaiah 41:10

What if I told you that during my time in The Land of Sand I led three people to the Lord? In my testimony, I would tell you how I prayed for them for years. How I lived "life-on-life" with them. How I cried with them and they cried with me. How I nourished them with the Word of God and taught them how to love Jesus. What if I told you that I took them in as part of our family; that we met daily and I taught them how to pray and how to memorize Scripture? What if I said that over a period of many years I never gave up on them and I taught them, by example, how to share their faith with other people? What if their lives were forever changed because of the time I poured into them? Would you be impressed? Would you wish you had the same opportunity? Would you secretly think, *Well, I wish I could do that, but I can't. I have children and I need to stay home with them*? Would you believe me if I told you that the same opportunity could be yours? Would you take me seriously if I told you that those three disciples were my kids?

We mothers have an amazing opportunity. We have live-in disciples! We are called to accountability in the way we act all day long and in every idle word that slips from our lips. Those little disciples are watching us! Don't ever think that you are missing out on ministry during your years of raising little ones. That's the most intense discipleship there is! Take pride in the opportunity to wipe that disciple's sticky face and gather up the energy to sing one more verse of "Jesus Loves Me," because that little one is listening to you and the words are going down deeper than you think!

When the boys were tiny, I tried hard to saturate their waking hours with God's Word. I had cassette tapes for the car and cassette tapes for the house. I helped them memorize verses from the Bible and tried to bring them up in daily conversation. I wanted them to see that God and His Word are a relevant part of life.

One day I had my two toddlers in the car with me and I was attempting to get my car from a stand-still on the dirt shoulder of the road to a fast speed among cars racing past us on a paved highway. I'd recently been working with the boys on Isaiah 41:13. From the back seat I could hear my oldest nervously pray out loud, "Oh Lord, hold our hand!!"

Another day, while still working with the boys on verses from Isaiah, I saw my younger son apply a verse to his daily life. I overheard an altercation in another room and went to see what had happened. My oldest looked hurt and my youngest, chubby cherub that he was, looked guilty. He admitted to me, "I hit him with my righteous right hand..." pause, "and my leftist left hand!"

Your "disciples" are watching you! They watch to see how you handle a bad day. They watch to see if you remember to thank the Lord for the things He gives you. They will not be taking notes with pen and paper, but the lessons they learn from you are written in their hearts with indelible ink. Take your Mom-Discipler job seriously and with humble pride. There will always be lost people to share Jesus with when your kids are grown up, or even, if you have any energy left, while they are taking a nap later today. But those disciples who are living with you now won't always be there. Enjoy your time with them now! You have an amazing ministry right in your own home. On that note, if your Little Disciples have left you alone long enough to read, you had better close this book and go see what they've been doing with their little "righteous right hands!"

A Collection of Verses

"Fear not, for I have redeemed you; I have summoned you by name; you are mine. When you pass through the waters, I will be with you; when you pass through the rivers, they will not sweep over you. When you walk through the fire, you will not be burned; the flames will not set you ablaze. For I am the Lord, your God, the Holy One of Israel, your Savior. Do not fret because of evil men or be envious of those who do wrong; for like the grass they will soon wither, like green plants they will soon die away. Trust in the Lord and do good; dwell in the land and enjoy safe pasture. Delight yourself in the Lord and He will give you the desires of your heart. Commit your way to the Lord; trust in Him and He will do this; He will make your righteousness shine like the dawn, the justice of your cause like the noonday sun. Be still before the Lord and wait patiently for Him; do not fret when men succeed in their ways, when they carry out their wicked schemes. Refrain from anger and turn from wrath; do not fret – it leads only to evil. For evil men will be cut off, but those who hope in the Lord will inherit the land. A little while, and the wicked will be no more; though you look for them, they will not be found. But the meek will inherit the land and enjoy great peace. God is our shelter and strength, always ready to help in times of trouble. So we will not be afraid, even if the earth is shaken and mountains fall into the ocean depths; even if the seas roar and rage, and the hills are shaken by the violence. There is a river that brings joy to the city of God, to the sacred house of the Most High. God is in that city, and it will never be destroyed; at early dawn He will come to its aid. Nations are terrified, kingdoms are shaken; God thunders, and the earth dissolves. The Lord Almighty is with us; the God of Jacob is our refuge. Come and see what the Lord has done. See what amazing things he has done on earth. He stops wars all over the world; he breaks bows, destroys spears, and sets shields on fire. 'Stop fighting,' He says, 'and know that I am God, supreme among the nations, supreme over the world.' The Lord Almighty is with us; the God of Jacob is our refuge." I praise You Lord because "As soon as I pray, you answer me; you encourage me by giving me strength. The Lord will work out his plans for my life – for your faithful love, O Lord, endures forever. In Thy presence is fullness of joy. I will both lie down and sleep in peace, for You alone, LORD, make me live in safety." So, "let us run with perseverance the race marked out for us. Let us fix our eyes on Jesus, the author and perfecter of our faith, who for the joy set before him endured the cross, scorning its shame, and sat down at the right hand of the thrown of God. Consider him who endured such opposition from sinful men, so that you will not grow weary and lose heart...May the Lord direct your hearts into God's love and Christ's perseverance. Now may the Lord of peace Himself continually grant you peace in every circumstance...He Himself is our peace."

Isa. 43:1b-3a; Psalm 37:1-11; 46; 16:11; Hebrews 12:1-3; 2 Thes. 3:5, 16; Eph 2:14

Day 8: Grace

Praise our God, O peoples, let the sound of his praise be heard; he has preserved our lives and kept our feet from slipping. For you, O God, tested us; you refined us like silver. You brought us into prison and laid burdens on our backs. You let men ride over our heads; we went through fire and water, but you brought us to a place of abundance. Psalm 65:8-12

It is a painful thing to be hurt by an unbeliever. It is another thing entirely to be hurt by a fellow believer. Of the many challenges and opponents to the spread of the Gospel, being hurt by "one of your own" may be the most difficult experience of all. For me, the deepest scars were carved into my heart by people I trusted. I am learning to use the scars as reminders of God's grace. The challenge for all of us is to never let the scars that each of us carry be kindling for a consuming fire of bitterness. If it ever becomes so, we will find ourselves to be the ones that are consumed. I want to look at my scars and, when I see them, I want to smile at the opportunity to talk about God's grace!

God's grace is not only for the Muslim, who is bound by the lie that salvation comes by works. Grace is also for God's children, who can learn to live by it and fall on it and thank Him for it every day! There was a time in our ministry when we had been deeply hurt. Our confidence had been stripped away. We felt very alone. Each morning it was a matter of the will to pull ourselves out of bed and keep going. We sought the Lord earnestly and dwelled in His Word. We were hurting, confused and mostly just very sad. Psalm 118:13 and 14 were literally my testimony: "I was pushed back and about to fall, but the Lord helped me. The Lord is my strength and my song; he has become my salvation."

I learned some important lessons during that difficult time. First, I began to learn for myself that there is truly "no condemnation for those who are in Christ Jesus" (Romans 8:1). Psalm 130:3 and 4 blessed my soul deeply: "If you, O Lord, kept a record of sins, O Lord, who could stand? But with you there is forgiveness, therefore you are feared." The Lord forgives us! His grace is what compels us to fear and worship Him! No one could stand before Him if it was about how good we are. But it's not. Oh praise the Lord! Down here in the world of imperfect humans, there are a lot of folks keeping records of what a lot of other folks are doing wrong. It's as if we are all walking around with clipboards in our hands grading each other. What a silly thing to be doing! It doesn't matter what we think of others or what others think of us! Paul says, "If I were still trying to please men, I would not be a servant of Christ" (Galatians 1:10). And then there's that teaching from Jesus about the man with the plank in his eye who is judging the man with the speck in his eye (Matthew 7). It seems pretty clear in Scripture that we have no business judging others; and, if we ourselves are being judged by others, we have no obligation to succumb to their verdict. We stand before God alone. Isn't it ironic and completely amazing that the only One who has any right to judge us is the most Gracious One of all? He is just waiting to pour grace upon us, even when those around us are eager for judgment! "What, then, shall we say in response to this? If God is for us, who can be against us? Who will bring any charge against those whom God has chosen? It is God who justifies. Who is he that condemns?" (Romans 8:31, 33, 34).

Another lesson I learned was about confidence. "So do not throw away your confidence; it will be richly rewarded. You need to persevere so that when you have done the will of God, you will receive what he has promised" (Hebrews 10:35-36). There are so many times, when living in a place like The Land of Sand, that believers are tempted to lose their confidence. No one ever steals it from us, however. We choose to throw it away. That is our choice. We are encouraged in Hebrews to hold on tight to our confidence. There is a great need for us to persevere. Hang on to your confidence in and through Christ, my friend. If you are spending time daily in the Word and in prayer, then, when you "hear that voice" in your heart throughout the day, you can trust that you are hearing from the Lord. Don't let anyone blur your thoughts and talk you into throwing away your confidence. It is your choice, so you hang on tight and trust your relationship with the Lord.

On the other side of a very dark season for us, I can look back and see how the Lord sustained us. I didn't come through without scars, but I am learning to make those scars reminders of the truly amazing grace of our God.

"Surely God is my help; the Lord is the one who sustains me" (Psalm 54).

I Wish

I wish it was not, but it is.
I wish it was easy, but it's hard.
I wish it made sense, but it doesn't.
I wish I knew why, but I don't.
I wish I understood, but I can't.
I wish it was short, but it's long.
I wish it was simple, but it's complicated.
I wish it were someone else, but it's me.
I wish it were over, but it's somewhere in the middle.
I wish it didn't hurt, but it does.
Yet, in spite of all my feelings, I know You are faithful.
I know You are with me.
I know You live and in the end You will stand and I will see You with my own eyes.
You know the way that I take and You will bring me out more golden than before because I will know You in a deeper way; a way I've not known You before.

(Job 19:25-27; 23:10)

Day 9: Gently Led

He tends his flock like a shepherd: He gathers the lambs in his arms and carries them close to his heart; he gently leads those that have young. Isaiah 40:11

"If I am going to spend all my time taking care of our babies, I can do that in Texas! I don't have to come all the way to Africa to do that!" Have you ever wondered what in the world you were doing in a "crazy place like this," wherever that may be for you? I knew that God had called us to Africa, and I knew that He had blessed us with children, but how in the world did those two combine in a way that was pleasing to Him? I didn't even have time for my "Daily Quiet Time," for crying out loud! God is our Shepherd, and He says that He "gently leads those that have young." God understands that a new mom is going on about 2 hours of sleep. God is gentle, He is not condemning us. Praise the Lord! He has mercy on those that have young!

During the years that I had little ones in my arms and toddling around my ankles, I would place small devotional-type books and copies of the Bible in different places around the house. I had some by the chair where I would nurse the baby. I had a couple on my bedside table. There was a devotional book in the kitchen, in the TV room, anywhere that I thought I might possibly spend more than a minute or two. Then, if the little ones were playing nicely, I could quickly and quietly grab a book or Bible and have a few moments with the Lord. This saved me having to go searching through the house for a Bible. Inevitably, by the time I found one, the kids would be ready for a snack or a nap or a diaper change or a scenery change. Nothing makes a child need his mom more than the possibility that his mom may actually sit down and relax a bit! During those little snippets of time with the Lord, He was so faithful to speak to me and refresh my heart.

We were newly in The Land of Sand when we began visiting a poor family across town. I enjoyed practicing language and getting to know this family that the Lord had placed in our lives. I remember getting frustrated when one of our children would distract me so that I could not pay attention to the conversation. One day in particular, one of our sons, a baby at the time, was crying and crying. He would not be comforted. I carried him outside and was walking around the yard singing "The Lord's Prayer." In my heart, I was wondering, "Why, Lord, is he crying so much? He is taking me away from these people that I want to be with." When I finished singing and the baby had calmed down a bit, I turned to see the wife standing there. She had been listening.

"What are you singing?" She asked.

"Oh, this is the prayer that Jesus taught to his disciples," I began. From there I was able to share with my friend a little about Jesus and what he taught. I knew in my heart that God had answered my question to him. My baby boy was not taking me away, but rather, the Lord was using him to put me in a situation where I could share Jesus with my friend.

If the Lord has blessed you with children, then He has also called your children to serve Him alongside you. Look for the ways He is already using them to bring honor to Himself!

Sineeya Khudaar
(Vegetable Tray)

Any vegetables, here are suggestions:

3 carrots, chopped

7 potatoes, chopped

1 medium onion, chopped

2 cups green beans

2 bell peppers, chopped

2 zucchini, chopped

1 cup macaroni

3 tomatoes

6 cloves garlic

Oil

½ pound ground meat

Fry salted potatoes in oil, fry unsalted carrots. Set both aside. Boil green beans in salted water until cooked, then drain and set aside. Boil all other vegetables except tomatoes and garlic in salted water then drain and set aside. Make macaroni according to package directions. Stew and blend tomatoes. Brown meat in oil and then add garlic. Mix all ingredients together, adding some of the water used to cook the vegetables to moisten. Ready to serve immediately or you can put in a casserole dish and heat in oven.

Day 10: Culture Stress

You are worried and upset about many things, but only one thing is needed.
Luke 10:41-42

Though the fig tree does not bud and there are no grapes on the vines, though the olive crop fails and the fields produce no food, though there are no sheep in the pen and no cattle in the stalls, yet I will rejoice in the Lord, I will be joyful in God my Savior. The Sovereign Lord is my strength; he makes my feet like the feet of a deer, he enables me to go on the heights. Habakkuk 3:17-19

When people first move to a new country, they have culture shock. Some countries produce worse shock than others. The Land of Sand is on up there in the list of "shocking countries." Even after one has come to peace with the way things work in a country, "culture stress" returns periodically. Culture is not a shock anymore, but it is very stressful! So that's what hit me yesterday. Add to it that there were additional stressors going on (like being sick) and it made for a culturally stressing day.

I got up the energy to go to the store to buy a few groceries. I shop at a particular store on Fridays, solely because hardly anyone is there on Friday mornings and I can shop in peace. But a couple of weeks ago they hired a friendly, assertive guy (probably a refugee) who wanted to push my cart for me. I wanted to shop IN PEACE and be left alone, that's why I shop at that particular store. A couple of weeks earlier, this same guy and I had a slightly loud altercation that ended with me and him pulling the cart back and forth like a couple of kids fighting over a favorite toy. I had won, but I felt pretty bad about it. Yesterday, I saw him coming...oh no...I tried to look busy and keep a tight hold on my cart. He kept randomly organizing groceries just in front of me so he could jump into control of my cart. My ignoring him worked until he got between me and the milk cartons I was trying to get. He got them and almost got my cart.

"No! Thank you!" I said with a strained grin, clutching my cart as tight as I could.

"No problem!" said he, moving in on the cart.

"NO! THANK you!!" I retorted, grabbing my cart and pushing on down the aisle. Good grief, I just yelled at a poor refugee who is just trying to do his job! He left me alone until time to check out.

After getting the groceries in the car, I attempted to get in the driver seat and was accosted by the trash bag man who tries to sell me trash bags. I hate to hold grudges, but over a year ago I bought bags from this guy and they were the wrong size. So I didn't buy any the next time, but he got mad about it and parked his bicycle in front of my car so that I could not pull out. I was SO tempted to just knock the bike over with my big 'ole car, but decided it wouldn't be very loving. So, here I was a year later with this same irritating man. I kept smiling and saying no and finally, he walked away.

I decided I needed some fruit, but the men at the fruit stand always flirt with me and I can't stand it and decided I WOULD NOT stand for it because it is completely inappropriate and they just do it because they think we "foreign ladies" are immoral and I WOULD NOT buy from them anymore. But I had to shop at the vegetable stand right beside them because THOSE guys are very nice and respectful and I've given them business for several years and don't want to take my business away just because the guys at the stand next to them are too friendly. So yesterday I decided I had no energy to buy from the veggie man and hear the catcalls from the fruit men. I devised a clever plan to pull my car PAST the fruit man to a fruit stand about 30 feet down and just buy fruit from the car. I got my money all sorted out and ready and then rolled down my window and began to drive. As I passed the stands I could hear "HAABEEEEEBTEEEEE!!!!" from the fruit men. GOOD GRIEEEEEEEEF!!!! Fully frustrated I rolled up the window and pulled back out into traffic and drove home. Never mind, I didn't want my children to have healthy fruit to eat any way.

Culture Stress: it comes. But the good thing is that it goes away too. In the meantime, I need to find a place where I can buy some apples and bananas.

10 Things I Would Not Have Done Today If I Were Living In The USA

1. I would not have seen a camel riding in the back of a small pickup truck in the middle of town.

2. I would not have commented to the boys, "Wow, the Nile is really high these days."

3. I would not have gotten these directions, "Turn right at the building that was attacked by rebels in May."

4. I probably would not have seen an 18-wheeler straddling a median (although I suppose it could happen even in the USA).

5. My friend would not have said, "It's nice out this evening, let's get a drink and sit on the roof."

6. I would not have looked over said roof right into the squatty potty of the next door neighbor's roof-less bathroom (thankfully no one was using it at the time).

7. I would not have gotten ready to leave my friends' at 6:30 pm and then said, "Oh no, I can't go home for another hour, my road will be covered with picnic mats for the breaking of the fast."

8. I would not have thought, while nearing the turnoff to our village, "Oh, looks like they moved the dead horse off the side of the road."

9. I would not have had to double-lock my gate so that my friendly neighbors wouldn't come walking in my house while I was getting ready for bed (in Texas you could get shot for less)!

10. I would not have crawled into bed, exhausted, but smiling with memories of another entertaining day in the Land of Sand!

Day 11: Across My Path

Pray also for me, that whenever I open my mouth, words may be given me so that I will fearlessly make known the mystery of the gospel. Ephesians 6:19

When we first arrived in The Land of Sand, we had a four-year-old and a one-year-old. Running a household in a third-world country was a big challenge! There was the daily beating back of the desert that encroached on our property in the form of piles of dust and sand. There was the intense heat that we were so unused to. There were three meals a day to cook for the family, clothes to be washed, well, you know the drill. I was a bedraggled, culture shocked, frumpily dressed mom and wife. In the midst of all the adjustments, we found out I was pregnant!

I remember looking out at our closed-in yard. Like all the houses in town, our grass, lime trees and red rose bushes were surrounded by a tall cement privacy wall. The world was going on just on the other side of my wall. How could I be a part of ministering to the people around me with a baby in my belly, a toddler on my hip and a preschooler holding my hand? And on top of that, I had the worst morning sickness yet!

Somewhere between loads of laundry and yet another Kool-Aid spill the Lord gave me the wisdom to pray this prayer, "Lord, if You will bring people across my path, then I will be faithful to share with them." How the Lord would bring someone to me seemed about as impossible as a neighbor walking through that 10 inch thick cement privacy wall. But bring them He did.

Lana was one of the girls He brought across my path. She was taking an English course at a center next door to our house. Between classes she would cross the street to buy a soda at the little corner store. A few times I saw her as I walked by and I would wave and greet her. Eventually, we began to talk and a friendship grew. Lana began stopping by the house to get a drink of water before or after her class. We would visit and she enjoyed talking to the children.

My preschooler, and I began to pray for Lana. He asked me if Lana was a Christian. When he found out she was not, he insisted that I needed to share about Jesus with her. After several days of this, I finally told him, "Let's pray for Lana. If you will pray for her, then I will tell her about Jesus."

The next time Lana came for a visit, my son wasted no time in reminding me to share with Lana! Talk about being held accountable!

After we had been friends for some time, Lana told me this: "My friends and I would talk about you when you passed us at the store where we were drinking sodas. You are the only foreigner who has ever bothered to greet us as you walked by. But, we assumed that you were probably not a good person. We knew you probably cheated on your husband while he was away at work." Wow! Talk about some scary assumptions! Lana continued, "But now, I have been in your house with you. I have been watching how you treat your children. I have seen how you treat your husband when he comes home from work. You have never told me with words, but I know for sure that you are faithful to your husband and you are a good mom."

People are watching us, no matter if we are walking down the street or if we are mothering our toddlers at home. I can testify that God was faithful to bring across my path the people whom He wanted to draw to Himself. He brought people to me, in spite of my privacy wall and morning sickness!

The Eid Song

It took me years to remember which Eid was which. Here is a song to sing to the tune "O Tannenbaum" to help you remember!

Oh Ramadan oh Ramadan

I'm scared to drive in Ramadan

Oh Ramadan oh Ramadan

I'm up at five in Ramadan

The call to prayer goes off and then

I can't go back to sleep again!

Oh Ramadan oh Ramadan

When will you end oh Ramadan?

Eid alFitr Eid alFitr

You wear new clothes at Eid alFitr

Eid alFitr Eid alFitr

Candy and cokes at Eid alFitr

Bring candy and you'll be a joy

And for the children bring a toy!

Eid alFitr Eid alFitr

The fasting's over and it's better!

Eid al Adha Eid al Adha

I love to eat at Eid al Adha

Eid al Adha Eid al Adha

There's lots of meat at Eid al Adha

Except raw liver I will eat

Most anything and it's a treat!

Eid al Adha Eid al Adha

I love to eat at Eid al Adha

Day 12: Kara's Baptism

For surely, O Lord, you bless the righteous; you surround them with your favor as with a shield. Psalm 5:12

Yesterday I sensed God's pleasure. Obedience always makes Him pleased! I cleaned the bathroom and Kara put a scented candle on the edge of the tub. We were happy to see that the water filling the bathtub was somewhat clear. In the kitchen, I made a fruit drink from instant powder. Together, we counted out enough tea glasses to set on a tray and prepared another tray for the bread. Both Kara and I felt a little giddy. Around 6:30 that evening, Alex asked if he could come in and pray over the bathtub. Alex is our night guard. He stays up most nights praying over our house, our neighbors, even our pets and trampoline! I told Kara that as long as she knew that the water was just plain water, nothing special about it, I didn't mind Alex praying over it. He knelt beside the tub and prayed for the upcoming event.

An hour later, we found ourselves squished into the bathroom. Twelve of us all together, we surrounded the tub. Jon, a national pastor, read a passage of Scripture and explained what baptism was all about. A couple of people were asked to pray. Then Kara sat in the water-filled tub. To be modest, she wore several layers of clothes topped by black pants and a dark shirt. Jon helped her lie backwards to immerse herself as a sign of her new life in Christ.

"In the name of the Father, the Son, and the Holy Spirit," said Jon. When Kara came out of the water we all clapped and congratulated her. She was so excited! Everyone went to the salon (sitting room) while she changed her clothes, but I stayed behind a few minutes. She wanted her picture taken and then we hugged, wet clothes and all!

"This is the second time in my life that everyone gathered in the bathroom," she said. "Do you remember? I told you about the first time." Indeed I did remember. Six months ago, Kara's family, upon discovering her new faith, cut off her hair, beat her, stripped her of her clothes, and forced her into the bathroom. Her whole family gathered in the bathroom and tried to force her under the shower to wash her in a Muslim ritual that would make her Muslim again. They tried, but failed, to rid her of the new "evil spirit" inside. When she refused to pray a Muslim prayer, they beat her more. The men of the family met in the salon to discuss her future. They decided on sending her to a "khalwa" where sheikhs (Muslim leaders) read the Qur'an to the students, often shackling their ankles and beating them with large wooden prayer beads until they were either "healed" or went mad.

Yesterday was the second time people gathered with Kara in the bathroom. This time, it was not her natural family but rather her new spiritual family. It was not a desperate act, but an event that had been prayed about and anticipated all week. She was not forced into the bathroom. Rather, she was the one inviting others to join the celebration with her. Instead of resisting, Kara willingly and happily participated. Rather than the shame of having her hair cut off and her clothes stripped away, Kara carefully selected an outfit from the collection of clothes freely given by her sisters in Christ. Instead of trying to cleanse her with water, those gathered in the bathroom celebrated the fact that she was already clean through the blood of Christ and that this baptism was only a sign of what had already taken place in her heart. Instead of trying to wash the spirit out of her, we celebrated the presence of the Holy Spirit in her. Instead of being commanded to pray a Muslim prayer, Kara requested that she be able to pray aloud to Jesus. Instead of disowning her, we called her our sister and fellowshipped with her through the Lord's Supper. Instead of the men gathering in a separate room to discuss her future, Kara joined in a discussion of her future. The plan for her future involved religious training, but not a "khalwa." Quite the opposite, it involved Bible courses offered by a church. Instead of shackling her, the school could send a letter of invitation and a church could provide a place for her to live. Instead of a busted lip, swollen face and bleeding eye, Kara's face shone and her eyes twinkled. Yesterday, just like on that day six months ago, God was pleased with Kara. The first time everyone gathered in the bathroom, Kara had obeyed God. She did not deny Christ, she remained faithful. God was pleased. Yesterday Kara obeyed God again. She followed her Christ in baptism, and she remembered His death and resurrection on her behalf through the Lord's Supper. God was smiling. God is always pleased with obedience! Yesterday I sensed His pleasure.

Mahalabeeya (Rice Porridge)

2 pieces cinnamon stick

2 cups uncooked rice

4 cups water

1 cup raisins

1/2 cup peanuts (roasted and skinned)

1 cup almonds or other nut (chopped)

1 1/2 cups milk.

Boil rice and cinnamon in 4 cups water until soft (no need to cover the pot). Remove cinnamon sticks. While rice is cooking, soak raisins in hot water. Cook peanuts in hot water until soft. Add milk to rice. Cook and stir on low heat until rice begins to get mushy. Remove from heat. Add drained peanuts, raisins and nuts. Stir. Serve hot or cold with sugar to taste. You can keep a bowl of this in the fridge and take out a serving for a quick breakfast or snack.

Day 13: Granting Desires

May he give you the desire of your heart and make all your plans succeed.
Psalm 20:4

God gives us the desires of our hearts. But what if your desire is something like…a piece of furniture? For several years, I had wanted a buffet table to have in our dining room. We hosted a lot of large groups and a buffet would make serving food much easier. But, I knew we couldn't afford it. I was frustrated that "all I wanted" was a simple buffet to serve food on. It didn't seem like much to want, but I did not know how I would get one. Finally, I decided to pray about it. Pray about a piece of furniture? I told the Lord, "You know I want this but we can't afford it. If You would like to provide a buffet for me, I know You can." Even though we had no extra money, I knew the Lord would provide if He chose to. The day after I prayed, I went up to the school where my kids attend. I saw a sign posted for a bazaar in the community. At the bottom of the flyer I noticed it advertised that individuals could rent a table on which to sell things. Immediately, I remembered my prayer and I knew this was an answer from the Lord.

I immediately began to go through our house to find things to sell. We had accumulated a lot of things from people who had left The Land of Sand. Most of it was too good to throw away, too much to give away, was nothing that we really needed, and was looking very tacky, all piled up in one of our rooms. I was thrilled at the possibility of getting rid of the many boxes. I took this time to also "Spring clean" our whole house. By the time the date of the bazaar had arrived, I had over eight large boxes full of items to sell.

I knew someone who had purchased a hutch from a used furniture market for about one-hundred dollars. I figured that if I could earn about that much, then I could also find a used piece of furniture for my buffet. The bazaar opened at 10 O'clock in the morning. By 2 O'clock that afternoon I had earned close to four-hundred dollars!

Amazed and dazed, I planned a trip to the used furniture market. Shopping at the used furniture market requires patience, imagination, the

42

willingness to do some repair work and painting and a great sense of humor. Over the period of a few weeks, I plunged into shopping, bargaining and painting. I went with a friend or two on each trip to the market. They were fun and funny adventures, as most outings in The Land of Sand are, if you take a companion with a sense of humor! In the end, I had enough money to purchase: a buffet, a large chest of drawers, a kitchen table, a stool, two large coffee tables and a round dining table. All of this, plus paint and hiring a truck to deliver, still left me with close to one-hundred dollars. My buffet was painted and ready in time for Christmas! We hosted about 20 people for the day. It proudly held meats and vegetables and delicious pies for everyone to enjoy.

Looking back on the whole experience, this is what I see: I asked the Lord if He might give me a buffet. Here's what He gave me:

1. Opportunity to get rid of all that junk and to organize my own belongings

2. Four times the amount of money I anticipated earning

3. Seven pieces of furniture, instead of just one, and money to spare

4. Special "friendship moments" with four of my friends

Sometimes God's timing doesn't make sense to us. I wanted that buffet long before I actually got it. Why did I have to wait so long? Often, as in my case, it is because He wants to do much more than what we are asking for. I remember when my oldest son, was very small and we were in a department store. I had in my mind to take him to the toy section and buy him a special toy that he would really like. As soon as we walked through the doors, however, he saw the bubble gum machines and really wanted a quarter to buy a gumball. I remember our struggle as he begged for a quarter and I knew in my heart that if he could just trust me and move past those trinket machines, I would surprise him with something bigger and better. How often we, as God's children, get distracted by life's "trinket machines" and beg Him for small favors when He has in mind to take our breath away with something more than what we would even think to ask of Him.

How Hot Is It?

1. It's so hot, I sat in a chair someone else had just sat in and it was cooler than the empty chair.

2. It's so hot, I opened my back door to find a frog and a lizard waiting to come inside and cool off!

3. It's so hot, the flies are too hot to fly around. They just walk.

4. It's so hot, my child has a high fever and is still 20 degrees cooler than room temperature.

5. It's so hot, I spilt hot coffee on myself and thought, "Oh! How refreshing!"

6. It's so hot, I have to put tap water in buckets to cool off so my kids won't scald themselves at bath time.

7. It's so hot I don't even want to paint my fingernails because it makes them too hot.

8. It's so hot I don't have to light my scented candles in order for the wax to melt.

Day 14: Crying Over Cookies

Cast all your anxiety on him because he cares for you. 1 Peter 5:7

Cast your cares on the Lord and he will sustain you; he will never let the righteous fall. Psalm 55:22

Pink, blue, green, yellow, orange, red and white. Seven bags of squishy icing. Four dozen sugar cookies. Hours of designs. And I mean amazing designs, if I may say so myself. I'd used my new cookie cutters from the US to cut out an array of shapes. Ice cream cones, hearts, kittens, cars, flowers and a number of other shapes. I used Royal Icing to carefully decorate each one. I was going a little crazy. I do that when my husband travels for longer than a week. On this night he was flying out for two weeks. I was drowning my sorrows in beautiful cookies. While he packed, I decorated. By the time we fell into bed that night, I had a plastic container filled with dozens of prize-winning cookies. I decided I'd probably give some away as gifts. They were just too good to keep to myself.

My husband left in the wee morning hours to catch his flight. I stayed in bed. In fact, I was so surprised on that Saturday morning to realize that all three of my little guys were playing happily on their own and therefore I was able to sleep in. I enjoyed a leisurely wake-up (a golden moment for a mother of young ones) and then I sleepily padded out to the living room to see what my little angels were up to.

They were indeed playing happily. But one thing was wrong. The plastic container of cookies was sitting on the coffee table with the top sitting askew, as if it had been opened. My heart skipped a beat. I went to the coffee table and lifted the cover. Inside were all the cookies. None were missing. However, one bite was taken out of every single cookie. Every beautiful, hand decorated, prize-winning cookie now had one little boy-sized bite taken out of it. All my work! All my cookies! My reaction must have been a sight to behold. I burst into tears! My youngest two were clueless as to what the problem was. They smiled sweetly at me, immune to my tears. My oldest was mortified. Even though he was not the culprit, he knew something was very wrong with

45

Mom. The cookies were obviously a lost cause, so he immediately thought of something that might make me happy. He grabbed his books from school and set at the table to do his homework. So here is the scene: a container of cookies (one bite out of all 48) in the hands of a crying mother, one seven year old frantically doing homework, a four-year-old playing with toys (oblivious to the unjust tragedy) and a two year-old smiling and saying, "Mommy! You crying!"

Pretty pitiful, isn't it? Funny how others around here think I am a totally in-control sort of person. I have a reputation of not getting rattled by the things that happen around us. Whoever started that rumor has never seen me on the mornings of my husband's two week trips! And note that whoever made up the phrase "No use crying over spilt milk," did NOT say, "No use crying over half eaten cookies." Apparently it was very worth crying over. I could hardly speak to my youngest son for the rest of the morning, I was so mad. But by lunch I'd realized there was nothing to be done but enjoy all the cookies ourselves. They certainly weren't prize-winning any longer, but they were tasty. All 48 of them!

A Letter Home

Dear Mom and Dad,

So often I get caught up in what is overwhelming around me and forget to focus on God. Last night a large group of ladies gathered for one and a half hours of worship. This was a time spent to focus on HIM. A couple of ladies played guitar and several people prayed. We sang songs and then had prayer on Worship, Confession, and Thanksgiving. Next, we divided into smaller groups for more specific prayer. For me it was a very special time of worship. I felt drawn into God's presence and fed by Him. It was a special time of personal devotion. During the prayers of confession, the Lord showed me that I had been tricked by a lie of Satan. Recently I have said, "How can He give us gifts and then not allow us to use them? Or give us desires and then not fulfill them?" That was Satan tricking me into doubting God's goodness, even if subconsciously. I confessed that sin to Him. Last night, the desire to serve Him well in difficult circumstances became stronger than my desire to get out of difficult circumstances. It was such a joy to worship with all those women and to think that the Lord was receiving so much praise.

Next door to the house where we met there was a "bika" (a visitation for the family of someone who had just died). The contrast was unavoidable. Here we were, a group of women living in a Muslim land, yet so full of hope. There they were, turbaned men living in a "man's world" but with no hope. Another significant thing for me was that as I walked into the room where we were to meet, I saw that we were to remove our shoes. When I did, I looked down and saw that my feet were filthy! I was embarrassed but I pulled my long skirt down as far as I could and went on in. I was reminded that the Lord loves us to come to Him just as we are and we don't have to be clean or perfect first, He will be the one to cleanse us and sanctify us. He just wants us to come!

I also had another thought last night. It was the first time in a long time that I felt like I feasted on the Lord and didn't have to leave this country to do it. It struck me that so often we gripe about that lack of deep spiritual feeding here, just like the Israelites griped about having to eat simple manna while in the wilderness. While the "milk and honey" we get when out of the country is wonderful and is needed, the Lord knows just what we need while we are here and we should not be guilty of griping about the manna He sends us. As simple and "bland" as it may seem sometimes, it is the very food of Heaven.

With love,

Your daughter

Day 15: Cultivate Faithfulness

Trust in the Lord and do good; Dwell in the land and cultivate faithfulness.
Psalm 37:3 (NASB)

I've been thinking about the words "cultivate faithfulness" from Psalm thirty-seven. The psalmist encourages me to "Dwell in the land and cultivate faithfulness." Earlier this week, I replanted cuttings of the last plant that survived our move to the new house in the "hilla" (village). It was actually a plant that belonged to a good friend of mine who had finished her contract and returned to the States. The plant was dying right at the stem, so I cut off five pieces toward the top and replanted them. Of course, if we evacuate, my plants will die. Talk of evacuation seems to be a part of life here. We have often made packing lists of things to bring should we have to leave quickly. More recently, we have actually packed bags with changes of clothes and our important papers. I knew that things were getting tense the other night, when I discovered that our house mouse had reserved her own spot in my "to go" bag!

We had been trying to catch a mouse in our house for a couple of weeks. We'd see evidence in the kitchen that a mouse had been rummaging around for midnight snacks. The mouse itself, however, remained elusive. One night, while my husband was away, I was lying in bed reading a book before turning off the light. I noticed some movement out of the corner of my eye and I looked across the room. There, on top of our "to go" (evacuation) bag was a mouse! I am not sure if it speaks more to my fatigue that day, or to a new level of low standards that I had arrived at that I simply threw a tarha (head scarf) at the mouse (who easily dodged it), then flipped off the light and went to sleep. The next morning I looked in the bag. Sure enough, our little house mouse had chewed up the extra change of clothes and a few papers (even a 10 Euro bill!) to make a little nest. I knew evacuation must surely be imminent if even the mice in the village were making preparations to be on the next plane out!!

So, why was I out in our hosh (outside area) carefully cutting and replanting and watering my new little plants? Somehow replanting those cuttings and carefully watering them each day reminded me to invest in

49

the days that I do have here, no matter how few or how many they are. As I got my hands dirty and repotted, I was thinking to myself, "My time here in The Land of Sand is for cultivating faithfulness: faithfulness to God…faithfulness to His call in my life…faithfulness to my family…faithfulness to my role in the work here…faithfulness in prayer…faithfulness in the daily tasks of living…faithfulness to share Christ." My five little plants may shrivel and die next week, if we evacuate…or I may have the time to plant and watch a tree grow in The Land of Sand! I have no idea how much time I'll have here. I need to leave that to the Lord and just water my plants (the real and figurative ones) every day…cultivate faithfulness!

I Had Hoped

I had hoped things would work out better: that colleagues would be more faithful, that leaders would be more effectual, that life would eventually get easier and that day to day living wouldn't be so arduous!

I had hoped to freely live out my vision, my dreams: that conflict would be resolved; that others would share my convictions; that a life of ministry wouldn't be so perplexing and that living out my faith wouldn't be so demanding!

So I prayed for change…and waited…and prayed…

I felt so empty: nothing changed.

I prayed and I waited, but all was the same.

Then, I realized that life is just like that: that wavering colleagues challenge *me* to be resolute, that fallible leaders stimulate *me* to strive for excellence, that sometimes life gets harder each day that I grow deeper in the Lord!

Then, I remembered that I should commit my vision and dreams to the Lord: because conflicts will arise as long as I am around other people, because others won't always agree with me and that will challenge me to broaden my perspective, because a life of ministry is very messy, because living out my faith is down-right hard!

The very agitations that seemingly hinder me are, in reality, the catalysts that work to mature me.

I feel so full, though nothing has changed.

I still pray, I still wait, but I'm no longer the same.

Day 16: Living Near the Gates

"And I tell you that you are Peter, and on this rock I will build my church, and the gates of Hades (hell) will not overcome it." Matthew 16:18

We are entering Day Ten of what is certain to be the longest dust storm in the history of hovering dust storms. I haven't seen the sun except for when it looks like a hazy moon somewhere on the other side of this orangey grey blanket that envelops the city. Some days bring just a light coating of silty dust throughout the yard and house. Other days, like today, the sand and dust left on the ground in the mornings is so thick that you have to sweep a path from the door to the gate. This much dust is annoying, frustrating, depressing and sometimes downright oppressive. Severe dust storms can turn the sky completely black, as if there was a solar eclipse.

I knew it was coming today because last night I was watering my potted plants. I ladled water out of a large plastic barrel and carefully refreshed each pot, watching the water fill the cracked soil. I stopped momentarily to clean my foggy glasses, only I realized they weren't foggy, it was the darkening air around me that was full of dust. Ah, yes, a thick dust storm was on its way.

I had prepared for the "haboob season" as we call it, the time of year when the dust from the desert around us kicks up and blows into town. I'd purchased weather stripping in the local market and done my best to seal all the windows in the house. While this helped some, nothing can hide from the dust of a haboob! Every item in the house shimmers with the golden dust. Clothes in the closet, food on the shelves, electronics…nothing is sacred!

It reminds me of the religion of most of the people here. Sometimes it is annoying, frustrating, depressing, and sometimes downright oppressive. I remember one day in particular when the oppression really got under my skin. In true drama queen fashion, I thought to myself, "I am very sure that this country is actually physically located right beside the gates of Hell itself." Thankfully, the Lord is not thrown off-track by my awesome drama skills. The Holy Spirit immediately reminded me of a verse and I went to look it up. There it was, Matthew 16:18, "And I tell you that you are Peter, and on this rock I will build my church, and the gates of Hades (hell) will not overcome it." Wow, even if this country really were located just beside the gates of Hell, God's church will not be overcome. But I'll tell you who was overcome by that thought...me! It doesn't really matter how bad things seem or how hard things get, God's church, His will, His victory will not be overcome. Praise the Lord! I posted that verse in my kitchen where I could see it and remember God's power in the midst of my drama.

Blogging

Once upon a time there were three little boys, a broken generator, and a husband who was gone away on a long trip, and a young mother. Okay, okay...it was me. Our boys were young, the littlest one still nursing, and my husband had to travel out of the country. In our dusty little home in the desert, when he "got to" travel outside the country, I always fought jealousy...and things always went wrong. On this particular trip, the generator broke.

We had a generator for the frequent power outages. At 120 degrees, once the electricity went out, it was only a matter of seconds before we were sweating and tearfully praying for the power to return. In the mean time we'd crank up our old half-working generator. Sometimes it worked. On this particular day it did not.

So the first scene that pops into my head is me sitting on the bed trying to nurse my baby. It is hot as you-know-what and I am dripping sweat. The last thing I want is a warm little baby body up next to me and I can't understand why my baby would want to drink milk at a time like this. Logic, of course, flies out the window when one is hot! I can't help but imagine his little baby belly full of curdled milk.

The second scene that comes to mind is later that day. I can't get the generator to start and am about to go out of my mind with the heat and three little heat-struck young'uns. I call the generator company in town and use my very best Arabic to tell them the problem. The man tells me that since I had a friend look at the generator before calling them, the warranty is void. WHAT? I explain that my friend didn't touch anything on the generator but he maintains that the warranty is now no good.

"You had someone else look at it, that is the problem," he says to me in Arabic. And here is proof that our deepest feelings can only be expressed in our heart language: because I burst out in English, loud English, angry English. I am pretty sure the loud and angry part translate pretty well, even if the words do not.

54

"THAT'S not the problem!" I say, my voice escalating, "You know what the problem is? The problem is my HUSBAND is gone and I am HOT!!!! And I have three little boys and THEY are HOT. WE NEED THE GENERATOR TO WORK!!!"

Those of you who know me can see the humor in all of this, as I have never yelled at a single soul. But that day, I found my limit! So here is my limit: 120 degree heat, husband gone, a preschooler, a toddler, a nursing baby, no ceiling fan, and news that my warranty is void. That's my limit y'all, now you know.

As bad as I felt about the yelling episode, it did get the results I wanted. The man paused for a second and then replied in Arabic, "We will come right over."

They honored the warranty and fixed the generator. We got some air circulating in the house. I did not hurt anyone, we all survived! I felt a mixture of accomplishment that I'd figured out a way to fix the problem and guilt that I'd resorted to yelling at someone to do so.

So what do we learn from that? I guess I learned my limit. That generator man learned not to mess with foreign ladies who are suffering from the heat! And maybe we can all just learn to laugh at ourselves a little more. I started, now it's your turn! Laugh at the crazy things you've done when you reached YOUR limit!

Day 17: But...

The weapons we fight with are not the weapons of the world. On the contrary, they have divine power to demolish strongholds. We demolish arguments and every pretension that sets itself up against the knowledge of God, and we take captive every thought to make it obedient to Christ. 2 Corinthians 10:4,5

We had been living in The Land of Sand about 2 years when we returned to the United States for a few months. We had been hit hard, both emotionally and spiritually, by the rigors of the ministry there. We'd experienced what seemed like an overdose of challenges. It seemed as if, when we got to the point where nothing else could possibly go wrong, about five more things instantly did! I remember thinking, "This place will chew you up and spit you out and never look back at you!" That's how we felt when we arrived on US soil: chewed up and spat out!

I made an important discovery during our time in the States. Not everything is The Land of Sand's fault! I found that my default, so to speak, was to blame things on the country we lived in. I was reminded that my passport country is not exactly a problem free country either. Now, don't get me wrong! I thoroughly enjoyed our time in the good 'ole US of A. But I also was reminded that the battleground is not necessarily the physical soil we walk on. Often the battleground is in our minds.

Now I don't mean to say the battle is made up - an imaginary thing. It is real. It is very real. But the battle is not the country you live in, it's not the people you work with, it's not the culture you are trying to penetrate. The battle is spiritual, and, because of that, the battle is often a battle in our minds.

We have been blessed to be a part of an amazing community of unified believers in The Land of Sand. But unity has not always been the reality of work among believers in The Land of Sand. During times when we were dealing with disunity or with team issues of various kinds, my husband and I were determined to "take captive every thought." We would hold each other accountable to the words we said, even in private, because we knew our words reflected our thoughts. Our emotional and spiritual workout plan, during those times, was to capture our thoughts (and words) and make them obedient to Christ.

I am encouraged by the words recorded by David all through the Psalms. He was very honest with his hurt, his confusion, his anger. But he always affirmed his belief that God was Sovereign through all of his experiences. In Psalm 22, David was overwhelmed and frustrated. In verse three, however, he says, "*but* thou art holy" (King James Version, emphasis mine). In the midst of it all, God is holy.

The author of Hebrews, in chapter two, verse eight, promises that everything is subject to Jesus, even while saying that "at present we do not see everything subject to him." He follows this with what I think is a very powerful statement: "*But* we see Jesus" (emphasis mine). We know that Jesus is the Victor in the end, however, we struggle to live victoriously in the "now." True, we do not yet see everything subject to Him, but we see *Him*! That is all we need.

Jehoshaphat had a similar attitude towards the Lord. He and his people, by human standards, were in an impossible situation. Jehoshaphat was alarmed, but he made an important decision in 2 Chronicles 20:2. He "resolved to inquire of the Lord." All of Judah fasted. Jehoshaphat did not ignore the impossibility of the situation. He admitted it to the Lord. In verse 12 of the same chapter, Jehoshaphat said, "For we have no power to face this vast army that is attacking us. We do not know what to do, *but* our eyes are upon you" (emphasis mine).

David, Jehoshaphat and the author of Hebrews all had the same mindset. Their words expressed this attitude: "I am in the midst of trials and confusion and impossibility...*BUT* God is holy, I see Jesus, and my eyes are upon Him." Oh that we would make our thoughts obedient to Christ and take up the same battle cry in the midst of our own life storms!

How Dusty Is It?

1. It's so dusty that wiping the dust off my Bible means I haven't read it in a couple of hours.

2. It's so dusty, I can write my name on every surface in the house not long after I've dusted it.

3. It's so dusty, the inside of my mouth feels dusty

4. It's so dusty, my face is chap from how many times I've washed the dirt off.

5. It's so dusty I hose my Christmas tree down before I decorate it for Christmas.

6. It's so dusty I suggest that my kids make sand angels on the front porch.

7. It's so dusty you have to remove the first tissue from a tissue box to find a clean one before you blow your nose.

Day 18: Build Your House

So I say, "My splendor is gone and all that I had hoped from the Lord." I remember my affliction and my wandering, the bitterness and the gall. I well remember them, and my soul is downcast within me. Yet this I call to mind and therefore I have hope: Because of the Lord's great love we are not consumed, for his compassions never fail. They are new every morning; great is your faithfulness. I say to myself, "The Lord is my portion; therefore I will wait for him." The Lord is good to those whose hope is in him, to the one who seeks him; it is good to wait quietly for the salvation of the Lord. Lamentations 3:18-26

There was a time when we thought we would be moving our family out of the city and to a small town several hours away. I could hardly contain my excitement. For me it was like a dream was coming true. I'd wanted to live in a small African village for such a long time. After months of preparation and for multiple reasons the plan fell through and we were not able to go. I was heart-broken. I felt lonely in my personal disappointment, because most of my friends didn't understand why I wanted to go to the village in the first place! As I often do when I need Scripture to saturate my day, I began to write Bible verses on note cards to post on the wall.

Isaiah 41:9-10 "I took you from the ends of the earth, from its farthest corners I called you. I said, 'You are my servant'; I have chosen you and have not rejected you. So do not fear, for I am with you; do not be dismayed, for I am your God. I will strengthen you and help you; I will uphold you with my righteous right hand."

Isaiah 41:13 "For I am the Lord, you God, who takes hold of your right hand and says to you, Do not fear; I will help you."

Jeremiah 29:11-12 "'For I know the plans I have for you,' declares the Lord, 'plans to prosper you and not to harm you, plans to give you hope and a future. Then you will call upon me and come and pray to me and I will listen to you. You will seek me and find me when you seek me with all your heart. I will be found by you,' declares the Lord."

As I read through these Scriptures, I was drawn back to Jeremiah 29. This chapter contains a letter that Jeremiah wrote to the exiles taken away to Babylon. Something that he said to them spoke to me. These people were living their worst nightmare; they were being taken away from the city of Jerusalem to live in exile. Surely they were mourning and wondering where God was in the midst of this tragedy. They probably hoped this would be a quick and temporary situation. Here is what Jeremiah said to them beginning in verse 4:

"This is what the Lord Almighty, the God of Israel, says to all those I carried into exile from Jerusalem to Babylon; 'Build houses and settle down; plant gardens and eat what they produce...Increase in number there, do not decrease. Also, seek the peace and prosperity of the city to which I have carried you into exile. Pray to the Lord for it, because if it prospers, you too will prosper.'"

I was in exile in a city too! I wanted to be in the small town. Through this passage I was reminded that:

1. It was God who allowed us to remain in the city and not move out.

2. He wanted me to "build my house" and settle down.

3. He wanted me to build my ministry in the city; to increase, not to decrease.

4. He wanted me to seek the peace and prosperity for the city He put us in.

5. He wanted me to pray for the city.

I was beginning to learn the secret of finding contentment and joy in Christ alone, not in physical circumstances. Therein lay the joy of life that seemed so elusive to me. Until God released us from this ministry, I desired with all my heart to choose joy and contentment. I determined to "build my house," even though it was not in the place I would have chosen.

99 Flies

Do the flies drive you crazy like they do me? I walk into the kitchen to cook dinner and the first order of business is to grab the fly swatter and kill a good twenty or so flies. The cooking that follows is interrupted by intervals of fly killing. To keep myself from getting mad about it, I made up a song to sing! Here is my song, to the tune of "99 Bottles":

How many flies can I kill at a time?

How many flies can I kill?

Slap them down

Dead on the ground

There is no end to the flies all around!

Day 19: The "P"s

Many are the plans in a man's heart, but it is the Lord's purpose that prevails. Proverbs 19:21

Why do some things work and why do some things not work? Sometimes I feel like I have such great ideas and wonder why they don't work out! For about a year and a half we lived outside the city in a village setting. Our house was situated off the dirt road just a bit with an open area that had an empty two-room building. I thought that it would be fantastic to start a neighborhood children's club. I had figured out that we could ask our landlord for use of the empty building. Perhaps he would approve, since it would be for the betterment of the neighborhood. I also imagined a women's group that could meet there. I'd already arranged in my head how I could recruit a team to clean up and paint the inside walls. In my mind it was a great ministry...and perfect for me, an at-home mom! It makes perfect sense...right? I thought so! That's not the only idea I have had. I've had all sorts of ideas ranging from simple ideas to huge projects. When I prayed about them, my prayers often went something like this, "Lord, this is a great way for You to show Yourself! It would be great for You to bless this idea of mine!"

It's hard to know exactly why the Lord allows us to do some things and does not allow us to do others. It is the mystery of following His will in all things! In looking at some of the ministries and projects that have truly been blessed of the Lord over our time in The Land of Sand, I have found a few common threads.

Prayer

Prayer is the first common thread. I believe prayer should be before and after and all through any projects that we participate in. I have been encouraged so much by the prayers of people all over the world on behalf of The Land of Sand. I have been blessed to see people come from far-away places in order to physically stand on the dusty soil and pray. I have seen how the Lord raises His people to pray for projects in the early stages that, later, have had great spiritual impact.

Presence

Many times there is a presence in an area or among a people long before there is fruit to be seen. The Lord calls His people to be a light for Him in many dark places. I am so thankful for the many brothers and sisters of various nationalities who are living in difficult places. This is His love in action! We are called to be a presence for Christ. I find it interesting that Paul, in 1 Corinthians 16:8,9, stays in one place (presence) because, "a great door for effective work has opened to me, *and there are many who oppose me*" (emphasis mine). He didn't let a little opposition from the enemy scare him off. He made it a reason to stay. We have all of eternity to live among the saved with Christ in Heaven. Let's spend our time on earth living among the lost so that we can invite them to meet Jesus.

Perseverance

Prayer and a presence, however, are in danger of falling short if there is not persistence, perseverance. We must be persistent in prayer, in courage, in hope. We must persevere even in the many challenges that arise. There may be many days, or many months or many years that we must persist. I have seen the Lord bless where His people have not given up. They have persevered. Hebrews 12:1 encourages us to "run with perseverance the race marked out for us."

Let us be faithful in prayer. Let us be a presence that honors Jesus. Let us be persistent and persevere in the work He calls us to. Let us make plans for sure, but ask for His purpose to prevail.

Before I Met You

Before I met you, all I could see was dirt and dust. It was everywhere on the ground and even blowing through the air and piled up on the sides of the street.

Before I knew your name, all the names ran together. I couldn't remember who was who because you all looked the same, and that "same" was very different than me.

Before I heard your voice, I heard a thousand other voices and the language was so different and the words spoken so quickly that I could not understand the meaning.

Before you served me hot tea, I was scared to drink or eat anything for fear of the infamous lurking Giardia that might attack my unaccustomed belly.

Before I shook your hand, I had never felt like this; like God was using me to touch a person whom He longed to save.

But, after I became your friend, I couldn't see the dirt and dust, not even the bits smudged on your face.

After I knew your name, I couldn't get it out of my head. I prayed for you and talked about you and asked others to pray for you.

After I heard your voice squeal in delight over my feeble attempts at your language, I became emboldened to try harder and learn more. The unfamiliar sounds separated into words and the words formed into meanings in my mind.

After I drank your tea, no one else's would do! I love the way you put just the right amount of cinnamon and cardamom into the water before adding the tea leaves. How did I ever enjoy plain tea before?

After I shook your hand, I couldn't let go. God is using me to love you. I have reached for your hand but God has allowed you to reach into my heart and now you will always have a place there.

Before we met, our lives were worlds apart. After we became friends, our hearts intertwined. I will not forget you. I cannot leave you without a piece of me being torn away. Funny, how one so foreign to me could become so transforming in me. I will never be the same.

Day 20: A Fishing Story

Then Jesus said to Simon, "Don't be afraid; from now on you will catch men." So they pulled their boats up on shore, left everything and followed him.

Luke 5:10b-11

Simon, James and John: here were men who loved to fish. They fished at night, they cleaned their nets in the day, they had their own boats, and they loved to fish. They must have been discouraged the night they caught no fish after hours of trying. They must have been tired and frustrated that their efforts had brought forth no fish. No fish meant no money or food to bring home to their families. Fishing was their livelihood. Then a man came and asked to use their boat. Simon, ever the knee-jerk reaction kind of guy, jumped into his boat and took Jesus out into the water a bit. Perhaps he hoped to earn at least a small fee for renting out his boat. Did he pay attention to Jesus as he spoke? Could James and John back on the shore hear Him? Had they heard about Jesus? Were their hearts pricked by His teaching? Perhaps he perched on the side of the boat and mended and washed his nets. After he taught, Jesus told Simon to go out and cast his nets again. Had Simon been planning to go home and take a good long nap, trying to forget his unsuccessful night? But into deeper waters Simon went, not without clarifying to Jesus that he had already tried all night long! He cast his nets and had the most success he'd had…ever! He had to call James and John to come help because his nets were ripping under the weight of a miraculous load of fish. They came and loaded up and then both boats were sinking with success! Talk about a big fish story!! There was no need to exaggerate around the dinner table tonight! Their fish story was all the Gospel Truth!! Can you imagine the fear, the excitement, the disbelief all rolled into the magical minutes of hauling two boats full of financial success back to the shore!? What was going on in Simon's mind?

"I can bring dinner home tonight after all!" "I can earn untold amounts in the market today!" "I can pay off my boat!" "I can repair the roof on my house!" "I can give my fishing buddies a bonus this year!" Did he wonder how he might convince Jesus to stay and be their

66

fishing consultant? He probably would have enough money now to give a handsome salary package! As they struggled to get their boats safely back to shore, was he mentally preparing a strategy on how to sort through all these fish in order to get them all to the market while they were still fresh? Did Simon realize that this guest in the boat was really no fisherman at all, and did he worry that Jesus would just get in the way of wrapping up this successful fishing trip, no matter how amazing He was? Was Simon wondering what in the world to do with Jesus once they got back to shore while he himself was swamped with the work that needed to be done to get these fish to market?

Whatever was going through Simon's mind at the time, here's what he did: he fell on his knees before Jesus. Whatever thoughts overwhelmed him, the one that brought him to his knees was this, "I am unworthy."

But the really surprising part of this story is yet to come.

The amount of fish they caught was awe-striking (v9), amazing enough to strike fear in the hearts of hearty fishermen (v10). This was the biggest success Simon had ever had, and had he an ounce of business sense, his mind would have been racing with ideas on how to make this success continue. His luck had finally turned! He was the best fisherman there ever was! And then came the statement that had the potential to change his life even more than a boat busting at the seams with the catch of a lifetime.

Jesus said, "From now on, you'll be fishing for people!" Have you ever heard a crazier statement? After hours of amazing intelligent teaching followed by the biggest miracle Simon could have imagined, this stranger uttered the most ridiculous statement. Here is Simon, on his knees bowing before a most awesome person, and then that person babbles a statement that doesn't even make sense. "Fishing for people? Do you even see what is going on here, Jesus? I am in the middle of the biggest success in my life, I am about to be famous, rich and very, very happy. Don't you want that for me? Isn't this what I've always dreamed of, what any level-headed fisherman would want? Don't you want me to finish this amazing day of fishing before you ask me to even consider anything else?"

But perhaps these are just MY thoughts, because Simon Peter's actions certainly did not reflect any of these questions. As soon as they got those wobbling boats to shore, those soon-to-be-famous-and-rich fishermen left everything….EVERYTHING! Those two fishing boats, the nets they'd just spent the morning washing and repairing, the most amazing catch their village would ever see…and followed Jesus who had just predicted the most ridiculous job change ever. Here are two boats that have cut deep wedges in the sand because of their weight, fish are flopping in and over and out of their wooden sides. Two boats are sitting alone on the seashore. Their owners are gone. Who would leave their boats full of fish? Why would no one stay to claim the prize of such an amazing catch? But no one is to be seen. Simon and his friends are long gone. They have followed the One who gave them the success in the first place. They have trusted the Man who seems to say that these boats of fish are just a shadow of things to come.

If Simon would speak into this situation, he might say something like this, "Why did I do it? I don't know exactly. All I know is that, though the words did not make sense to me at the time, I knew they were from the Master… MY Master… and I was compelled to follow. I had to trust that whatever this man Jesus had in mind, it was far better than the best success I'd had. I had to trust that leaving behind those fish was the wisest thing I could do. Do I regret it? No way! Sure, I don't know what might have happened had I stayed behind and held onto my boats full of fish. Maybe I'd be rich and famous. But I would have no part in the Kingdom of God. And somehow I know, deep down, that saying yes to two boats full of fish would have meant saying no to countless souls. That day in the boat, I knelt before a man I'd never seen before. I was surrounded by flopping fish. Because of a simple choice I made that day, I kneel before that same Jesus, now crowned King of Kings, and, instead of flopping fish, I am surrounded by countless believing souls all gathered with me to worship Jesus the Christ. Instead of a sea of gurgling water, I look out over a sea of praising believers. I traded success for service to the One True God. I traded fish for an eternal family. I traded a fishing boat for life with Christ. I traded nets for knowing the Truth. I traded the catch of my life for Eternal Life. And I have never regretted the trade."

Bits and Pieces

* Speaking Truth is a privilege. We are the salt of the earth. Make your conversations salty! Have a celebrative spirit, not just in the times that someone believes the Truth, but also in the times you get to share the Truth!

* When I first left home to go to high school in a far-away city, my mother gave me a postcard. It was a postcard from Hawaii and it was of a surfer riding on a large wave. On the back she had written these words: "Ride the waves of your circumstances, don't drown in them." Ever since then, I've had a postcard of a surfer to remind me of her advice. Don't let circumstances beyond your control drown you, learn to ride them!

* A long time ago a counselor gave me some advice: When you are in a tough situation or are tempted to feel depressed, read humorous books and also write letters (or do some other thing that forces you to think of others.) I have found these two activities to be very helpful, especially when we lived in a pretty isolated area.

* Celebrate little victories! You may have just ridden a rickshaw all by yourself. You may have just said your first full sentence in your new language. Good for you! Don't qualify it or down yourself for what you did NOT do. Celebrate what you DID do! In the same way, celebrate with others. Congratulate them for their little victories.

Day 21: Re-entry

O Lord, you have always been our home. Psalm 90:1 (GNB)

More than anything else, however, we want to please him, whether in our home here or there. 2 Corinthians 5:9 (GNB)

Living in the United States is not all it's cracked up to be. Now, I can't say so to my friends back in Africa. And the reason I can't is because I know what their reaction would be if I did so. It would be the same reaction that I had when any friend of mine went "back" to the States and complained. Here is what my reaction would be: "Are you kidding me? At 100 degrees inside this house, I can literally feel the sweat rolling down my sides under my long sleeved blouse that I am wearing with my long skirt as I sit in a dust covered chair twitching my feet to scare the flies away. The only reason I can read this email you are writing me is because I have five minutes left on my dying computer battery which I won't be able to charge again until either the electricity comes back on or the generator gets fixed. I am spending these five precious minutes to read an email from you that says that America is hard because your stomach hurts from all the rich food and that you have way too many choices? Really? You are going to write that to ME?"

Actually, the States is great, especially if you are just passing through! You can enjoy the food, the great shopping, family and friends and many modern conveniences without the hassle of trying to fit in! This time around, though, we are stopping long enough to put the children in school.

On the boys' first day of school we parked in the parking lot and walked them in. On their second day of school, I was on "bus duty" and the boys said they were ready to be dropped off like the other kids. So, when 7:30 am rolled around, we piled in the van and drove to school. I was very careful to slow down to 20 miles an hour when entering the school zone. Then, I turned right at the entrance and circled into the school drop-off section, carefully maneuvering into one of the two lanes of cars dropping off kids. When our turn came, we stopped at the crossing guard and the boys hopped out. The oldest boy shut the heavy sliding door and they trotted off to the building. I began to pull out until the guard grumpily stopped me because it was not my turn to go just yet. Flustered and embarrassed I also noticed that the sliding door was not properly shut. Suddenly, the guard waved me on and I pulled up to the school exit which had a red light. While worrying about the barely-shut sliding door, and still embarrassed about my premature start at the crossing guard, I looked up and noticed that the two lanes had narrowed into one exit lane on the right so that the left lane (which had a green light) could be the entrance. I was now in the lane of entering traffic and there was a car stopped in the middle of the intersection trying to get in, except I was in the way! I mouthed largely through my windshield "I AM SO SORRY!!"

Mercifully, the car in the right lane stayed back long enough for me to make a sharp right turn and pull out of the parking lot, though now I was going in the complete opposite direction of my house. Finding no place to pull over to fix the van door, and trying desperately to get away from the car following close behind (whose driver had seen everything), I darted into a gas station and stopped. The car behind me (that I was sure had a driver who was shaking his or her head and tisking at me), drove on past the station. I sighed in relief and then crawled to the back to re-shut the door. It was then that I noticed four dollar bills in my pocket. Good grief! I'd forgotten to give the boys their lunch money! Back to the school I went and parked in the parking lot. I hoped the grumpy crossing guard did not recognize me as I slinked by him on my way to the front office.

Through all of this I was completely embarrassed and felt as if I must have a big sign on my forehead that read "I don't know any of the rules around here and I have no common sense!" I was very happy to get back to the house and hide indoors for a few hours!

I expected to have funny stories about my social faux pas in foreign countries. Somehow it wounds my pride a bit more to experience them in my passport country! The question runs through my head, "Is there no place that is my home, where I know how things are done?" Well, it certainly brings to mind the words of the hymn I used to sing with my family as a kid, "This world is not my home, I'm just a-passing through. My treasures are laid up, somewhere beyond the blue. The angels beckon me from heaven's open door, and I can't feel at home in this world anymore!"

71

The Greatest Trial

The greatest trial of the desert

is the fearsome heat

That blows in yearly with the dust

as if to compete.

The people wilt, the donkeys sigh,

the sheep will sadly bleat.

This trial converges on everyone

from poor to the elite.

The greatest trial of the desert

blows hotly down the street.

It melts the candles, scalds the water,

burns the grass and wheat.

The power cuts, the masses grown;

all sweat from head to feet.

Kudos to those who, with a smile,

survive the summer heat!

Day 22: All In A Day

We loved you so much that we were delighted to share with you not only the gospel of God but our lives as well, because you had become so dear to us.

1 Thessalonians 2:8

The beginning of my day finds me sitting in the humble home of Haya, a refugee from a war-torn area. She eagerly welcomes me while her teenage daughter, Lena, brings me the customary cup of cold water. I thankfully drink the whole thing. It is getting hot these days and I appreciate the refreshment; wondering only briefly if the water is filtered or if I will get diarrhea from it. I have come to bring Haya's family an Easter gift. I have prepared a small Easter basket with shiny confetti, candy, a Bible Story puzzle for the children, and a small copy of the New Testament. Four-year-old Ahmed snatches the New Testament and won't let go. Two-year-old Abdu grabs the confetti and candy, squealing in delight. The two teenaged kids work on the puzzle. Everyone, including Haya, is huddled over the Easter gifts, taking pleasure in each little part of it.

Haya's husband comes home from his work at the bakery to eat the customary eleven O'clock breakfast with his aging father. Lena prepares a tray of food and Hamid, the teenage son, takes it to his father and grand-father who are sitting around the corner in the men's section of the house. A few minutes later the tray, returns and Lena prepares to serve the leftovers for us. Haya invites me into a room with a dirt floor that has beds against three of the walls and a small TV against the fourth. I sit on the edge of a bed while Haya sits on a stool. The tray, with the leftover breakfast, is placed on a small coffee table between us. The grey putty-like mound of dough on the tray is not fresh and the outer layer is dry and crusty where it should be soft. The tomato gravy poured over it is slimy but tasty. As I press my fingers into the crusted-over pile of dough and dip the blob into the slimy red gravy, I try not to think about the fact that two men have just eaten out of the same dish with their hands and that we are eating their leftovers. Ahmed and Abdu join us, since the tray is right at their hand level. The four of us enjoy the fellowship of a shared meal together. A few minutes after the boys join us, I begin crunching on the grit that was added to the food by Ahmed's sand covered hands. I whisper a prayer, asking the Lord to relax my gag reflex.

After breakfast Lena brings me a cup of tea and Haya shows me photos in a tiny photo album. It is her way of letting me into her life and I am thankful. I sip my tea, tickle Abdu (who giggles and wriggles), tell Ahmed he is so smart as he works on the puzzle, and watch as the New Testament travels around from Lena's to Hamid's to Haya's hands. I pray that the words they read will pierce their hearts. My heart is full. I love spending time with poor people.

The end of my day finds me in the home of Halimah, a wealthy lady who invited me for tea. Tea, however, turns out to be a table laden with salads and meats and vegetables: amazing culinary delights with excellent presentation, as well as taste. A maid helps her with preparation. Her children and my children are watching satellite television, playing video games and enjoying soccer in the beautiful garden outside. After eating, Halimah and I sit in the air-conditioned living room and drink tea out of fancy tea cups. I notice that there is a Bible in her bookshelf. I pray that the words will pierce her heart. My heart is full. I love spending time with wealthy people.

I am blessed to experience the hospitality of a humble refugee at the beginning of my day and a wealthy business woman at the end of my day. Both are loved by the Lord. Both have His Word in their homes. Both have filled my heart. I pray that the Lord will fill their hearts.

The Underground

A cute blue gingham skirt it was,
Hitting just above the knee.
Flippy, flirty cotton dress
It really felt like "me."

I was proud to look so cute,
I fairly floated down
Those concrete stairs that led me to
The London Underground.

What I didn't know that day
Was what lay just ahead
And if I'd known, I'd have stayed at home,
Or worn blue jeans instead!

Vacation with the family
Was what I headed for.
A week in London! Shows and shops
And tourist sites galore!

The "Tube" they say, its silvery trains,
Is really quite a feat.
Transporting people here and there
Below the busy streets.

And here I was among the crowd
Excited to be there!
Bags in hand, I rushed to catch
The train to Russell Square.

The color coded maps direct
The travelers criss and cross.
I was so proud to reach my spot
Without even getting lost!

See! I could be a Londoner.
I know how to behave!
I fairly floated up the steps
And over a metal grate.

Now the Underground has vents, you see,
And this I did not know:
That wind blows UP those metal grates
Causing cute skirts to blow.

My skirt defied all gravity!
I put on quite a show.
'Twas my spontaneous impression
Of Marilyn Monroe!

Hands still full of bags, I ran
Across the grate, relieved
That no one saw my escapade…
Or so I did believe.

Until I heard a "WHOOPS!" and then
To my dismay I saw
A man working a newsstand
Hold his sides in a guffaw!

Indeed I gave a show that day,
Then to my hotel I went.
I promptly changed to blue jeans
And ne'er wore that skirt again!

You see the London Underground
Has "special" memories for me,
But one rule: no flirty skirts
No matter how cute they be!

Day 23: A Surpise Blessing

Always be prepared to give an answer to everyone who asks you to give the reason for the hope that you have. But do this with gentleness and respect

1 Peter 3:15

"MISSIONARY." Eeek! The word produces all sorts of interpretations from "crusader" to "spy," from "highest calling" to "worst enemy." It's no wonder that I hear the word less and less when we are overseas. As we raise our children, we are teaching them that all believers have a command from the Bible to share about Jesus wherever we are. It doesn't really matter about our vocation or location. It doesn't matter about our age either. We have taught the kids that if they are old enough to believe in Jesus, they are old enough to share Him and to pray for those who don't know Him yet. While teaching our kids what we believe to be biblical principles, we have not used the word "missionary" very much. I have discovered, however, that, back in our passport country, the word is still alive and in use. This was never more real to me than the day our oldest son learned the word.

We were in the States for a long enough time for our son to attend school and get involved in our church in Texas. He enjoyed the excitement of many new activities and opportunities. He made lots of friends. One night, after a Wednesday children's program at church, our son came home to tell me that the class was collecting food and canned goods for a missionary family. I was excited for the opportunity that my son had to learn about service. Here was a chance to look beyond ourselves, to give to someone else who was less fortunate than us. We were very blessed. We were living in a house rent-free and the church had even filled our cabinets with paper goods and groceries upon our arrival. Yes, we had been blessed by others and now our son would be able to be a part of blessing someone else in the same way.

The following week I gathered some groceries together for him to take to church. I filled a bag with pasta and beans, I even reached way back into the recesses of the pantry shelf for the can of beets we had been given that I knew I'd never use. Off went our son, bag of groceries in hand. I, his mother, smiled sweetly at the thought of my son learning about serving others.

An hour later, when his program was over, I went to church to pick him up. I saw him down the hallway as he made his way toward me. He looked confused. In his arms were sacks of groceries.

"'Turns out," said the bewildered boy, "WE are the missionaries!'"

So much for the opportunity to teach my son about serving others. We helped him get all the bags of groceries in the car. And yes, my sack with the can of beets was among them!

Salata Aswad (Eggplant Salad)

2 eggplant

1 carrot, grated

3 or 4 limes

1/2 teaspoon pepper

1/4 teaspoon salt

oil

2 Tablespoons peanut butter

1 Tablespoon water

1 tiny onion, chopped (optional)

Small can tomato paste (optional)

Peel and thinly slice eggplant, set slices out on a plate for 30 minutes. Fry in oil. Cool and mash. Mix together all remaining ingredients except carrots. Mix the "sauce" with the mashed eggplant and then add in the carrots. You can also add tomato paste or chopped onion.

Day 24: A Weighty Subject

But God's word is not chained. 2 Timothy 2:9

Lately, I have felt the need to carry a Bible in my purse, in case I have the opportunity to give it to someone while I am out and about. The Bible I have is a bit bulky and takes up quite a bit of space in my purse, not to mention that it adds quite a bit of weight. After several weeks of lugging it about, shoving it to the side to find a pen or some change, I'd begun to be a bit resentful of the burden. But last week I forgot about the hassle. I had to go across town to pick up our three boys, so I walked out to the main road and flagged down a rickety old yellow taxi with an old man driver. This taxi had no door knobs, no working dials on the dashboard, just two yellow wires sticking out. I'm not entirely sure there was even an ignition key involved. But the driver seemed like a nice man, and offered a good price, so I jumped in and off we went. Putt...putt...putt... Half an hour later we arrived, he was very cordial though and didn't say a word to me (which is respectful in this society) so I was pleased with him. When I loaded the boys in the taxi, he perked up. When my nine-year-old got in the front seat and greeted him, "Salaam Aleykoom," he was very impressed and went on and on about it, saying, "You said all the right words! You are Muslim of course!!" Then to me, "Are you Muslim or Christian?" to which I replied that I was Christian.

"Oh yes!" he said, "Christian! Esa (Jesus)! Mary!" I just sort of grunted. He asked my son, "Is The Land of Sand better or France?" I decided not to correct him on our nationality, as Americans are not necessarily liked by everyone here. My son said, "The Land of Sand" and again earned raving praises from the driver.

A few putt putts down the road, I decided to ask the obvious, just to get back to the religion topic, "You are Muslim of course?"

"Oh yes," said he, "but we are the same. Muslims and Christians are the same! We have the same prophets!"

"Have you read the Gospel?" I asked.

"A little bit."

"I have also read a little bit of the Qur'an," I said, "Esa (Jesus) is in the Qur'an."

"OH YES!" he said proudly. Forty-five minutes later we had putt-putted our way back home. He helped me unload the boys and all their stuff.

I handed him a little extra money and said, "This is because the traffic was so bad." Then I handed him the Bible and said, "and this is because you are a good man." He was thrilled to get it and thanked me several times for it. I went into our house and felt a noticeable difference in the weight of my purse. It made me think of the weight of my heart when I see lostness all around me. I long for the people around me to know about Christ and sometimes that heaviness is hard to bear. But I wouldn't want it any other way. Until Christ Himself returns, I want to carry with me the weight of the lostness, because I never want to forget to share Christ with someone. My heavy purse reminds me that I have something to share with those around me. And though I was thankful that my purse was lighter again after giving that Bible away, I went back in the house and put another Bible right back in it.

Lord, may I never set aside the burden of sharing with the lost, may I carry it with me wherever I go so that I will remember to share with those who need to hear.

I Was Thirsty

I was thirsty, so thirsty
And they came and dug a well, a water well.
I was overjoyed, so overjoyed.
My whole village was overjoyed!
Water! Imagine…no more carrying water
In jerry cans, so heavy, so heavy,
For kilometers of sandy paths under
The hot, hot sun.

I was sick, so sick.
My stomach hurt, my head hurt.
The fever burned and burned
My whole family was worried.
Help! My father brought me to a clinic.
The doctors were strange people from far, far away,
But they gave me medicine and I went home and felt
Better and better.

I was scared, so scared.
Men came rushing through on camels.
I was running, running.
My whole village was running.
Ratatat! Guns were firing.
Houses were burning, burning.
My village lay in ashes under
The hot, hot sun.

I was sad, so sad
They had killed and wounded so many.
I was afraid, so afraid.
My whole village was afraid!
Help! My own father was wounded.
Then I remembered, remembered
Those foreign doctors, the clinic…
Hope! Hope!

I walked and walked.
My father rode our donkey all the way.
There it is! There it is!
The clinic is here...help is here!
Why are the doors shut? Where are they?
The doctors are gone...gone.
I turn and lead the donkey with my father back home under
The hot, hot sun.

In 2009 many humanitarian aid organizations covering approximately half the aid in a war-torn area were expelled.

Day 25: The Valentine Gift

And I will do whatever you ask in my name, so that the Son may bring glory to the Father. John 14:13

We spent some time as a family in the United States when our oldest son was five years old. During the winter months, he prayed for snow. "Dear God, please, could you send snow here to the United States? I want to have a snowball fight and build a snowman." Every few days he wondered out loud why God hadn't answered his prayer. I didn't have the heart to explain to him that we lived in Central Texas and it just doesn't snow there much at all! He, however, was not deterred from his request to God, and he had no doubt that God would answer. One day, his younger brother decided to pray for snow as well. Distraught, our oldest son said, "He can't pray for snow too! God will send snow for my prayer and if He sends snow for his prayer too, then we'll have a BLIZZARD!"

The Friday before Valentine's Day was very cold. The weather man even predicted a small amount of snowfall for the afternoon. Our son was so excited, but I warned him that the snow probably would not stick when it hit the wet ground. Even as I did, a little voice in my heart said, "My child, your son is praying for snow and believing God will send it. What sort of image are you building in his mind of God and His desire to answer our prayers?" My boy had a solution for the "not sticking to the ground" problem. He decided we'd just catch the snow as it fell from the sky and make it into snowballs before it ever hit the ground. It did, in fact, snow just a tiny bit in the early afternoon, while he was at school. True to the weatherman's prediction, it did not stick. My son was sad.

"It was Valentine's Day, it was supposed to snow for Valentine's Day," he said. I bit my tongue after reminding him that actually Saturday was Valentine's Day. That night I talked to God and "reminded" Him that a small boy's young faith was hanging on to prayers for snow. In my heart, I was "reminded back" that this was between my son and God, not me and God.

84

That night, our younger son crawled into bed with me and I felt his little body hot with a high fever. He coughed and sputtered and had a hard time sleeping. I got up and gave him some medicine, but it didn't seem to calm him enough to sleep. As we lay in bed, I silently prayed and asked God to calm his cough. Usually, I give God my reasons why I think it would benefit Him to answer my prayer. For example, "God, this would really glorify You in the eyes of unbelievers," etc. That night it was just me and my son. No one would "see God's glory" revealed through a miraculous work in that little sick body. But as I prayed, I realized something. "Lord, this is not about You benefitting by getting glory. This is about You helping Your children because it's Your nature. You are Glory Itself. Please help this child because it is Who You are." And, yes, the Father did reach down and calm my son so that he could sleep quietly the rest of the night. Thank You, Lord.

The next day was Valentine's Day. My oldest son wanted to watch Saturday morning cartoons and I was helping him find the right channel. As I flipped past a weather show, we both noticed the pictures of snow in Dallas. "Man!" he exclaimed, "We should have gone THERE!" I was disappointed too, that it was snowing in Dallas and not where we were. Then I had a thought...hmmm... I peeked out the window and saw nothing but white! God had sent my son a beautiful valentine. The ground was full of several inches of fluffy white snow! We were able to bundle up and run outside for snowball fights, a huge snowman and several snow angels. I bet God looked down with pleasure!

My son had never doubted, so he was not surprised at his Valentine's Day gift, but his mother learned several lessons that week about God and His faithfulness to answer the prayers of those who believe (and even of those whose faith waivers a little bit). The next day my son said, "I wonder what God will give me NEXT year for Valentine's Day!" I resisted the urge to "protect" him from disappointment.

"Yeah, I do too!" I said. And in my heart, I truly believed that God would give us another great gift for Valentine's Day, not because we deserved it or because He needed the glory, but because that's just who He is!

Key – A Circle Poem

My parents, siblings and I have been somewhat spread out across the world over the past few years. E-mail has been a great way to keep in touch. Sometimes we share what we are learning in our Bible reading, sometimes we share poems or stories we have written. Sometimes we send out an idea or subject for others in the family to respond to. It's fun to see what the others have come up with. Recently, my niece sent out a "Circle Poem Challenge." A circle poem begins and ends with the same word. Each word between those two should have something to do with the word preceding it. My niece assigned the word "key." Immediately, Isaiah 33:6 popped into my head.

He will be the sure foundation for your times, a rich store of salvation and wisdom and knowledge; the fear of the Lord is the key to this treasure. Isaiah 33:6

Key

House

Foundation

Storehouse

Full

Treasure

Salvation

Wisdom

Knowledge

Fear (of the Lord)

Key

Day 26: Ahmed's Bibles

As the rain and the snow come down from heaven, and do not return to it without watering the earth and making it bud and flourish, so that it yields seed for the sower and bread for the eater, so is my word that goes out from my mouth: It will not return to me empty, but will accomplish what I desire and achieve the purpose for which I sent it. Isaiah 55:10-11

The Kingdom of God is growing and spreading. It does not grow and spread like we might think it would or it should. Ahmed learned that the Kingdom of God grows in ways that are mysterious and wonderful.

Ahmed had been in a North African prison for three days. On the first day, when police raided the worship service held in his home, many of his friends had denied their belief in Christ and had been allowed to return to their families. On the second day, after Ahmed and the others were beaten and forced to stare at the sun, a few more returned to Islam. Ahmed and his two remaining friends were tired and depressed. Ahmed's eyes ached and his vision was now blurred. His back and abdomen were bruised and sore from where the police had kicked him the day before. He had not slept well and the only food he had eaten since arriving in the small cement room at the police station was day old bread dipped in hot sweet tea.

Why was God not protecting him? Ahmed had felt sure that God Himself had been the One who had given him the idea to worship in his home. He had been very pleased at the number of believers who met with him each week to pray and read the Bible. Ahmed had even been able to secure enough Bibles for everyone to have their own copy and had extras for future members. He kept the Bibles at his home; mindful of the problems the members of his tiny church might have should they carry these Christian Books back to their own homes. If all of this had been God's plan, why was Ahmed now sitting in a hot prison? Why had those who denied Christ so easily been allowed to return home while Ahmed and his two friends had been beaten and abused? Wasn't God more powerful than man? Why was He not protecting Ahmed?

Ahmed was overcome by fear because of what lay before him this third day in prison. Each time the police summoned him for interrogation, they had threatened more beatings. But on this day, the police officer who interrogated him announced that after the customary mid morning breakfast, Ahmed and his friends would be shot in the courtyard unless they recanted their belief in Christ and returned to Islam.

Ahmed and his friends, trembling in their bodies and hearts, agreed not to deny Christ and to face whatever fate came to them that day. After the officers had eaten their breakfast, the three prisoners were lead to the courtyard. They lined up against a crumbling brick wall for what Ahmed could only assume would be the last memories he would have on earth.

While waiting for their executioner, Ahmed saw a stack of books on the ground across the courtyard. These were the Bibles that had been confiscated from his house three days ago. He could see that the police were preparing to burn them. Ahmed noticed a man walk by the stack of books, glance left and right, then quickly snag a book and slip it inside his jacket. Ahmed was amazed and looked about to see if anyone else had noticed. No one had seen! There was a flicker of hope in Ahmed's fearful heart. A few minutes later, still standing in the hot sun against the brick wall, Ahmed saw another officer walk by the stack of books, look about and then cautiously grab a small New Testament and slip it in his pocket. The flicker in Ahmed's heart burst into a realization. This was the reason for all that had happened. God was using Ahmed and his two faithful friends to distribute Bibles to security police!

A few moments later the executioner arrived, only, he had no gun in his hand. He escorted the three men to the head office where papers were stamped and they were released. There was no apology given for their incarceration and no reason given for their release.

Ahmed never saw those Bibles again and doesn't know if any of them got burned. He still suffers physically from the beatings he received during his time in prison. But he is thankful that God saw fit to let him distribute Bibles to security police. Ah, the Kingdom of God is growing, even in Islamic countries! *(Based on a true story)*

I Prayed For You

Today we sat on tiny stools and drank coffee
in a Muslim town...many bumpy miles away.
As we looked around, eyes open, one of us prayed.
We prayed for your freedom, did you know?
We prayed for your soul, dear woman.
Has anyone ever prayed for you before?
Has your soul ever been petitioned for
in the presence of Almighty God?
I looked into your eyes as I prayed:
Helpless soul, lost, unreached, untouched.
Did you feel anything? Anything at all?
As your eyes have pierced my heart
Will God's love pierce yours?
Will someone come to this town: hot, dusty, and undeveloped?
Will you see the True light?
Is this the only prayer that will ever be uttered on your behalf?
And then will you return to your way, a dark path?
Our eyes meet...
My heart breaks...
I'm praying for you.

Some place higher...better...many worlds away...will our eyes
meet again?

Day 27: Rain

If we are faithless, he will remain faithful, for he cannot disown himself.

2 Timothy 2:13

It was raining! I love rain! The thunder was rumbling, the wind was blowing and we were safe and warm inside. I was raised in the tropics of Southeast Asia and I LOVE the rain. Here I was living in a desert in Africa, and I was so pleased that I would still get to enjoy rain! I could almost smell the refreshment that it was sure to bring come morning. The rain was earlier than usual in this desert town, and the storm stronger than usual. There were sure to be a few broken limbs on the ground and items scattered in the yard by the strong wind.

We had not been in our new home very long and I was feeling culture shock. Everything was new and different and most things seemed very hard to deal with as well. Life was just rough there, and I was feeling a little battle-scarred. I felt that the rain was good for my soul. Like comfort food to a hungry stomach.

The next morning, filled with joy over the rain, I hurried to the front door. I threw open the doors, my mind already imagining the fresh green of the newly washed trees and bushes, the smell of grass and the damp, still, peaceful, warm "after-ness" of a beautiful rain. It was my first real "rain" experience of our desert country. And when I opened the door, I did not see what I expected...

Apparently the storm had taken the birds by surprise. When I opened the front door I *did* see our front yard, and it *was* washed clean of the dust, and yes, there *were* leaves and some broken branches. But mostly what I saw was dead birds. Dead birds were scattered all over our yard. One half-dead bird twitched at my foot right there in the doorway. I felt the most sudden and cruel fall from an emotional high to an emotional low. I couldn't believe it. Rain was supposed to be beautiful, but in my new home, it was HORRIBLE! Could anything be beautiful in this place?

Years later, after I had grown accustomed to the unpleasant rains in our town, I would joke with my national friend. We'd say that God only sent rain once a year to this country. Every "rainy season" He'd send rain and then the awful smell of trash and urine that stirred up in the muddy streets would rise to heaven and God would say, "Oh yes, now I remember why I don't send rain to that country!" Well, now, of course we didn't believe that story at all, but we enjoyed laughing about it.

While the rain had some benefits, it surely did have a lot of negatives, not the least of which was the awful stench and the city's lack of draining that caused lakes to form across the roads all throughout the city.

Never again did we experience the dead bird ordeal of that very first rain. But it will always be in my memory. I tell it as a funny story now, but at the time it was not funny at all. At a time that I felt so very low, there was still a "lower" to fall to. I often found myself in that situation. Just when I thought things couldn't possibly be worse, about five more terrible things would happen, leaving me feeling like the proverbial cartoon character with stars and whirls swirling around my head. The fact is, that even in those "lower than low" times, God never left me. I cannot testify to my faithfulness to Him in all things, but I can testify that He was *always* faithful to me, come rain or shine!

Ahlan, Baby!

The story is fiction, but the event has probably happened often in many countries like the Land of Sand.

I think today is the day. I am really scared, but there is nothing I can do to stop what is about to happen. I felt pains this morning that woke me, even before the call to prayer from the neighborhood muezzin. I lay in my bed and pulled the sheet over my head to hide from the flies that were awaking in the morning air. I could hear others stirring around me, all of us lying on metal framed beds out in the garden: my mother, my sister, and my two nieces. The men of our family were sleeping in the garden on the other side of the house. If I spoke quietly, I could tell my mother without waking the others. But I didn't. I was afraid that if I told her about the pains, she would say it was time to go to the hospital. I didn't want to go.

But now something strange has happened. Mother said my water has broken. I don't know what that means, but I feel like I peed all over the bed. Now the pain is even worse. My mother says not to yell if the pain gets worse. She says to stay calm and she will call the midwife. The hospital is too far away she says. I am even more scared. I know who the midwife is. She is the one that performed my circumcision when I was a child. She cut me and she sewed me up when I was only five years old. I remember it well. I don't like her, but now the pain is so bad, I don't have the energy to fight with my mother.

They have moved me to a bedroom now and my sister is wiping my head with a cloth. I am trying not to scream. My niece has gone to tell my husband, Nadr. Nadr and I have been married for one year. I live with him at his parent's house. It is very different there because his sisters do not like me. I am so happy to be at my mother's house for the birth of my baby. My baby! Oh, it hurts so much, what do I do? Make it stop! Out of the corner of my eye I see Khaltee Amna, the midwife. I know she will have to cut me where she sewed me up so many years ago.

I know my mother told me not to, but I scream anyway and all goes black…

******

It has been three days since my baby was born. I wish I had been unconscious the whole time. Unfortunately, I was awake for the cutting and the pushing and I did my best not to scream very much. A baby girl was born and I was so happy, but I heard Khaltee Amna say "Malesh" to my mother. "Too bad, better luck for a boy next time," she said quietly after she sewed my back up. It only stole my joy for a moment. For just a moment, my mother's face looked angry at Khaltee Amna, then her sweet smile came back and she offered the older woman some hot tea.

My sister came to attend to me. She gave me my beautiful baby girl to hold. I want to name her Maria, but I think Nadr will name her Fatima, a good, strong Muslim name. I hope Nadr is not disappointed that his first child is a girl. I have more chances to give him a boy. I hope no one else says "Malesh". I don't want to hear that again! I want to hear, "Mabrook!" "Congratulations!" There is still plenty of time to give him a baby boy. For now I will enjoy my baby girl! "Ahlan!" "Welcome, baby girl!"

Day 28: How Sweet It Is

How good and pleasant it is when brothers live together in unity!

Psalm 133:1

I maneuvered our car around the potholes of one of the paved streets in our area of town. All the streets branching off of this one were dirt roads with bits of pavement peeking out of the dust, remnants of tarmac from a previous existence. There was no drainage along the streets and roads of the city, so when the rains came, this road would be flooded with muddy water, making it impossible to miss the potholes. But it was dry season and the city was as bone dry as the desert that surrounded it. I passed the intersection where Legless Louie used to sit. For years that intersection was his place of work. I suppose a relative would set him there each morning because, even when I drove by in the mornings, Legless Louie would already be there. He was an elderly gentleman in a jallabeeya (white robe) and a brown tageeya, a skullcap-looking hat worn by many Muslim men. I never knew his real name, but we called him Legless Louie because he had no legs. He would sit at a T-intersection, but just a bit out in the road so that you had to be careful not to hit him as you drove by. He would hold Muslim prayer beads in one hand and beg from passersby with his other. Legless Louie always seemed to be in good spirits, and people walking by never seemed scared of him. He was there for many of the years that we lived there, but he was getting old, and I wondered how long it would be before he died. One year we went on vacation and when we came back, Legless Louie was gone. The intersection seemed so empty without him. My heart hurt when I thought about Legless Louie and where he was for eternity.

After passing the intersection where Legless Louie used to sit, I passed the Saudi Arabian embassy. Except for the impenetrable doors on the brick privacy wall and the large national symbol of two crossed swords and a palm tree in the upper space between them, one might not realize it was an embassy at all. Every time I passed it, however, I felt it represented so much more than just the embassy of a Muslim country. I would pray every time I passed, or would just start declaring in my car that Jesus is Lord!

94

About half a kilometer past the embassy was my destination. I made a U-turn and parked under a tree on the side of the road. I grabbed my container of brownies and my Bible. It was Tuesday morning. Every fortnight a group of ladies gathered for fellowship, Bible study and prayer. Sometimes this group of ladies felt like my very life-line. We were German, Dutch, and American. In the beginning it felt a bit awkward to me, like we were all "checking each other out" so to speak. After a few months of meeting, I really began to look forward to the time and I enjoyed praying for my sisters in Christ in between times. We prayed over each other through joy and through tears, and through the successes and struggles of our husbands in their work. I loved the fellowship of a group of ladies who were not all American. Though, I have to say, I was very thankful we worshipped in English. Those poor European ladies still had to fellowship and worship in a second language! When we were all together, I would try my very best to not be the "obnoxious American" that I often felt like Americans become when a group of them (us) get together. For me that was difficult because I was already an extrovert and quite talkative. But, as we grew closer, we were knit together and appreciated each other's differences and all we had to offer to the group.

Usually someone would play guitar and we would sing a few songs. Of course we didn't sound great, but our voices blended and the accents just made the melodies even sweeter. Women from different backgrounds all called to live in the Land of Sand for this moment in time. All of us desired to be devoted wives, caring mothers and dedicated followers of Jesus in a hot, dusty, Muslim land. Our differences melted away so that thoughts of denomination, culture and language were replaced by our desire to worship Jesus together

An African Paraphrase of the Twenty-Third Psalm

With the Lord as my guide, I will be in need of nothing.

Though I am surrounded by heat and dust, He lets my soul rest as if it were in a beautiful green meadow.

And though there is lack of drinkable water here, in the Lord, my spirit has an everlasting supply of fresh cold water that restores my dry soul.

Though here, one worries of land mines, the Lord sees the spiritual land mines that the evil one sets to destroy me, and I do not have to fear about them because the Lord leads me in my path.

Even though I walk through the desert of the shadow-less heat, I do not have to fear being overcome by evil, because You walk with me.

Though the tribal sword and stick look foreign to me, Your rod and Your staff are familiar and they comfort me.

Though I eat strange foods here, and long for the tastes of home, You prepare for my heart a feast of delicious foods when I come into Your presence.

You give me more than I need, and while I often feel overwhelmed by the differences here, I am also overwhelmed by Your goodness to me.

Wherever my life takes me, You will go with me, and at the end of my life, I will step through Your front door to live with You eternally.

Day 29: Bible Studies and... Other Things

A time to tear down and a time to build, a time to weep and a time to laugh.
Ecclesiastes 3:3,4

*Now, I don't like to just find a Bible verse to match what I want to write about. But I hope that through this "time to tear down" in my life we can all just enjoy a "time to laugh" together!

The next time you wad up a piece of paper and toss it in ole' File 13, remember your sisters in more...sensitive places around the world. I may never be able throw away things without remembering my trash fiascos in this desert home. When we were packing to leave our home for good, I came across several items that just couldn't be thrown away. That's normal, right? Everyone has private stuff that is not really for public consumption. How do you throw those things away?

Our first pile of private trash was about a zillion papers. Some were just personal in nature, some held financial information, etc. You get the idea. Thankfully, we had a paper shredder. Our paper shredder didn't like to work so hard, however, and it would overheat. My husband, my oldest son, and I spent hours shredding papers and filling large trash bags with the cross-cut shreds of confetti. Thinking this would be sufficient (I mean, you would think that was sufficient, right?) we sat the bags out on the side of the road with our neighbor's trash, hoping it would get picked up while we were in town. Late in the afternoon when we returned, and the image is forever ingrained in my memory, we rounded the corner to our little village home and it looked like the first ever Saharan snow storm. White flecks where scattered all over the dirt road by little kids who came to see what the white foreigners had thrown away. I was horrified and I am sure the neighbors were too! I saw some kids later trying to sweep up the mess. It was a hopeless cause, but I am pretty sure someone's dad made them try.

My second lot of litter was a stack of old Bible Studies. They were great studies, but I'd filled in all the blanks with my own private answers and thoughts. I had no room to take them with me and I certainly didn't want the neighbors using them to practice English. I couldn't shred them with our already overworked and dying paper shredder. It would take too long to rip them up by hand. Finally I filled a bucket with water and slid the studies right in. Talk about soaking up a good Bible Study! Literally. I let them soak until they were good and soggy. Then I ripped them in half, wadded them, tore them some more and basically made them unreadable. But now, full of water, they weighed a ton. So then I had to set them out to dry. THEN I threw them in the normal trash as dried up, sunbaked, shredded, soaked wads of...well hopefully no one could tell.

My third round of rubbish was some, umm...underthings. I didn't want them anymore, but they were also not quite the kind I wanted to hand out to the neighbors either. What to do? The paper shredder was out. Soaking them would not help. So I finally found a large metal bucket that I took outside. I dumped in my lingerie, poured a little kerosene on top and, yes I did, I burned them! They sizzled and smoked and I stirred them with a large stick to make sure the destruction was complete. Here's a little limerick I wrote about the experience:

There once was a lady in the village

Who did not want her trash to be pillaged

So she shred them and soaked them,

Sun-baked them and stoked them.

That crazy 'ole lady in the village!

Bible Verses the Lord Used to Calm My Heart

When it Was Time to Say Goodbye to the Land of Sand

Jeremiah 10:23 I know, O Lord, that a man's life is not his own; it is not for man to direct his steps.

Psalm 31:14-15 But I trust in you, O Lord; I say "You are my God." My times are in your hands.

Psalm 32:8 "I will instruct you," says the Lord, "and guide you along the best pathway for your life. I will advise you and watch your progress."

Psalm 33:10-11 The Lord foils the plans of the nations, he thwarts the purposes of the peoples. But the plans of the Lord stand firm forever, the purposes of his heart through all generations.

2 Corinthians 4:1 Therefore, since through God's mercy we have this ministry, we do not lose heart.

Day 30: Bookends

I know, O Lord, that a man's life is not his own; it is not for man to direct his steps. Jeremiah 10:23

But I trust in you, O Lord; I say, "You are my God." My times are in your hands. Psalm 31:14-15b

The "Land of Sand" experience is sandwiched between two bookends called your "coming" and your "going." How you "come" and how you "go" determines the middle part. Satan attacks strongly at both ends. Ironically, victory has nothing to do with the actual circumstances. Victory has to do with how we respond within those circumstances. I have noticed that the attacks to a person new in The Land of Sand are often strong and hard and often come early on.

My husband and I have been involved in the orientation of many folks to The Land of Sand. My husband even dubbed one of our sessions "The Jugular Talk." The enemy will attack us full on at our weakest link. He doesn't pick at us from the sidelines. He comes at our jugular with full force. What is your jugular? Don't be scared, but be prepared.

I have prayed often for new folks to have God's strength to just hang on and persevere through intense attacks early on in their experience. If they can make it through, a wealth of rich experiences and deep joys will be at the other side. If they give up, they will either leave the country defeated, or will hobble through their time in The Land of Sand, dragged down by bitterness, complaining and the inability to see any good in what is around them.

Now that our time in The Land of Sand is coming to an end, I am experiencing the heavy attack on the other end. Like bookends, the strong attacks on either end of the Land of Sand experience determine if your tenure will hold together or fall apart. Naturally, at the end of a term or segment of time, we tend to evaluate our work. Did we do well? Did we accomplish what God had for us? Were we faithful servants? Along with healthy contemplation come unhealthy questions: How do others think we did? Will our work be remembered? Will we be missed? Will our ideas and efforts be maintained after we leave?

Undoubtedly, Satan can use this time to cast false thoughts into our heads. "They are glad you are leaving!", "Everyone will carry on much better once you are out of the picture", "You were a failure here, better you just leave," on and on go the accusing thoughts. How we deal with the bookend called "going" works retroactively to determine how we view our time in The Land of Sand. I am learning that the end is just as critical as the beginning.

Initial entry into The Land of Sand is often overwhelming: heat, dirt, living conditions, health, expectations… everything is breaking, no one is fixing it…my life has just been turned upside down and everyone else is bustling about like it is no big deal. Whatever the circumstances are, our response determines what comes next.

In the same way, the circumstances of leaving The Land of Sand are somewhat irrelevant to the whole experience. Did you successfully finish your term or contract? Were you asked to leave by the government? By your sending agency? Did you have to leave due to lack of funds? Due to health problems? Family issues back home? The reason is irrelevant. The response is important. Lord, help us to have the grace to make it through this passageway called "departure." May we each make it to the other side in Your strength and do so gracefully!

As we prepared to leave, I became very sad as I packed and sorted through eight years' worth of stuff. I was struggling with all the circumstances that surrounded our own leaving of The Land of Sand. The next day, I talked on the phone with a young wife and mother whose family had just arrived in The Land of Sand. Their new house was a mess and had multiple problems. Adjustment to a new place with a young family is challenging in the best of circumstances. When you add heat, dirt, language barriers, Ramadan, electric cuts and a recent rain that leaves the entire city in a stinky puddle of suspicious muck, the stress level becomes almost more than one can bear! I found myself asking the Lord for grace for her to just hang on.

I am standing on the second bookend. While I pray for God's grace to make it through my own trials, I am cheering on the ladies who are teetering on the first bookend. "Come on, Ladies!" "Do it in God's strength, Ladies!" "Just hold on tight to Jesus, Ladies!"

God Himself should be the only One who determines how many "books" are between those bookends that begin and end your "Land of Sand" experience. Don't try to tamper with how many books are in there! Let God be the One who chooses the number. Let God give you the grace that sees you through the fiery bookends on either side, binding it all together to make your time in The Land of Sand the victory that He wants it to be!